The Encyclopedia of World Sports

by
John Wukovits

FRANKLIN WATTS
A Division of Grolier Publishing
Danbury, Connecticut
New York • London • Hong Kong • Sydney

Produced in association with Mountain Lion, Inc.

Writer: John Wukovits
Managing Editor: Mark Gola
Designer: Max Crandall
Page layout: Margaret Trejo

For Franklin Watts: Doug Hill

Library of Congress Cataloging-in-Publication Data
Wukovits, John F., 1944–
    The encyclopedia of world sports / by John Wukovits.
        p. cm.
    Includes bibliographical references and index.
    ISBN 0-531-11777-4 (lib. bdg.)   0-531-16134-X (pbk.)
        1. Sports—Encyclopedias, Juvenile. [1. Sports—Encyclopedias.]   I. Title.
    GV567 .W85   2001
    796'.03—dc21
                                                        00-038222

Photo Credits: Owen Franken/Corbis: 77. All other photographs were produced by AP Wide/World Photos except for those images appearing on pages: 3, 8, 9, 18, 19, 61, 62, 63, 65, 140, 149, 156, and 162. These images are the property of Mountain Lion, Inc.

Contents

Foreword

by Michael Freeman

I am a sports reporter and writer for *The New York Times*, the best-selling newspaper in America and one of the most widely read publications in the world. Our sports section, where my articles appear, is read by people from all over the planet: Argentina and Chile, England and Ireland, and Japan and Australia. We cover not just the sports familiar to Americans—baseball, basketball, football, hockey—but also sports that are most popular outside the United States: nordic skiing, bobsledding, hurling, curling and fencing, to name just a few.

Sports is truly a global community. Watch ESPN or other channels that broadcast sports 24 hours a day. You'll see men and women competing with and against one another in nearly every part of the world. To be a real sports fan today, you must keep up with the game people play everywhere, not just at home here in America. That's where this book, *The Encyclopedia of World Sports,* will help.

The Encyclopedia of World Sports is chock full of fun and fascinating information about nearly every sport you can think of. You'll find out how each sport started and was developed, what the rules are, its history and defining moments, who the great performers are, and which competitions are the most important. Want to know when and where speed skating started? It's in here. Want to know the names of the greatest thoroughbred race horses in history? It's in here. Want to know who is the most awesome discus thrower in Olympic history? It's in here. (His name is Al Oerter, by the way, and he won an amazing four Olympic gold medals.)

I have interviewed some of the greatest athletes to ever compete. People such as Michael Jordan, Joe Montana, Jerry Rice, Mia Hamm and Cheryl Miller. It's my job to be prepared for those interviews, to have my facts straight before I start asking questions. That's where a book like *The Encyclopedia of World Sports* becomes so valuable—it gives you the facts you need to speak intelligently about any sport. Whether you're trying to settle a friendly argument, answer a question from "Trivial Pursuit," working on a school assignment, or preparing for an interview with Tiger Woods, *The Encyclopedia of World Sports* is the perfect resource for finding the information you need.

Had it been available when I was a student back at Mount St. Joseph High School in Baltimore, Maryland, *The Encyclopedia of World Sports* would have occupied a special place on my bookshelf. Take it from a guy who covers sports for a living, this book is a sports fan's dream, a single, comprehensive resource for information about all the sports that people play.

Alpine Skiing

Alpine skiing consists of different downhill races. It combines speed, balance, and aggressiveness. The name Alpine comes from the Alps, the mountain range in Europe where downhill skiing started.

Equipment

Alpine skis are made from fiberglass, plastic, metal, or wood. They are narrow slats that curve up at the front end, or the *tip*. The ski's center is called the *midbody*. It is slightly raised above the level of the tip and the ski's end, called the *tail*. This makes turning easier. The skis also have metal edges along both sides for more controlled turning. The taller the athlete, the longer the skis.

Ski poles are used for support and body control. They extend from the rubber or plastic handle to a pointed end at the bottom. The point is surrounded by a circular or star-shaped piece of plastic called the *basket*, which prevents the pole from sinking into the snow.

Boots are fastened to the skis either with buckles or with cables and plates. Ski bindings hold the boots to the skis. To minimize the risk of serious injury, the bindings quickly release in case the skier takes a spill.

Alpine skiers may wear thermal underwear, a turtleneck sweater, insulated ski pants, a parka, gloves, and a hat.

The Event

Five different events comprise Alpine skiing—the downhill, the slalom, the giant slalom, the super giant slalom, and the parallel slalom. Skiers race individually in the first four events. In the parallel slalom, two skiers race

Trio of Styles

Downhill skiing has three basic maneuvers—schussing, traversing, and turning. Schussing refers to skiing in a straight line down the slope without turns or stops. The skier strives for speed only. In the traversing maneuver, the athlete skis at an angle to control his or her speed. Turning, either by holding the ski tips together in a wedge or by holding them parallel, enables the skier to change directions.

Andrea Mead Lawrence became the first American skiier to win two gold medals at a single Olympic Games.

head-to-head down identical courses. In the downhill and super giant slalom, the competitors ski down the slope once. In the other three events, they make two runs.

Downhill racing is held on a course with at least a 2,500-foot (750-meter) vertical drop. Skiers may select their own routes, but they must pass through control gates (parallel poles with flags). Top skiers approach speeds up to 80 miles (115 to 130 kilometers) per hour. The winner is the competitor with the lowest time in completing the course.

The slalom forces the athlete to navigate through a series of numbered gates. Officials plant the gates in spots that force the skiers to make numerous zigzags. The number of gates on a course can be as high as seventy.

The giant slalom combines the downhill race and the slalom. There are fewer gates (thirty or more) and they are set farther apart to permit higher speeds. Some parts of the course have no gates. The super giant slalom is similar to the giant slalom, but the course is longer, steeper, and has more gates. The slalom events combine all the skills of ski racing.

In the parallel slalom, two skiers race downhill side-by-side. The course forces the skiers to pass through twenty to thirty gates.

The best skiers train for the World Ski Championships, held every odd-numbered year, and the Olympic Games, which arrive every four years. Governed by the Fédération Internationale de Ski (FIS) worldwide and by the United States Ski Association, the sport has developed a loyal following throughout the world. Amateur skiing's most coveted trophy is the World Cup title, which is awarded to the skier who wins the most points in World Cup competition.

History

Skiing started thousands of years ago in the northern climates of Europe and Asia. Skis were first used by the Russian army in 1483, and came into widespread use in Europe shortly afterward.

Eskimos in northern Canada introduced skiing to North America in the early 1700s. Skiing appeared in Greenland in 1722. Norwegian immigrants brought skiing with them to the United States in the mid-1800s, but the sport did not gain widespread popularity there until the 1930s.

Meanwhile, the sport became very popular in Europe. The world's first ski competition occurred among Norwegian soldiers in 1767, and the first ski club opened in Christiania (now Oslo), Norway, in 1870. Norwegian athletes perfected downhill skiing, then introduced the sport into Germany, Austria, and Switzerland.

Two Austrians, Mathias Zdarsky and Hannes Schneider, developed techniques that improved skiers' abilities to control speed and to turn and stop. The sport's first big stride occurred in 1921 when Switzerland hosted the first organized slalom race. Three years later, skiing appeared in the Olympics, and the World Ski Championships started the following year.

A revolutionary change in the 1930s brought the sport to thousands of people worldwide. Resorts constructed ski lifts, which enable ordinary people to easily ascend slopes to enjoy skiing. More than one thousand ski resorts currently accommodate millions of Americans who have taken up the sport. Skiing is an excellent form of exercise, conditioning both the lower and upper body.

Legendary Italian skier Alberto Tomba in action.

Best of the Best

With the arrival of television coverage in the 1960s, skiers of Alpine events became known worldwide and emerged as the sport's first superstars.

France's Jean-Claude Killy—popular in part for his dashing looks—became an international star by capturing World Cup championships in 1967 and 1968 and three gold medals in the 1968 Olympics. Killy became only the second Alpine skier to win gold medals in the downhill, slalom, and giant slalom events. Following his triumph, he retired from competitive skiing.

Sweden's Ingemar Stenmark followed Killy and won eighty-six World Cup races in the 1970s and 1980s. Italy's Alberto Tomba set records in the 1990s.

Good balance keeps skiers from falling, but they must shift their weight from side to side to change direction.

United States skiers made their first impact in the 1950s, when Andrea Mead Lawrence, a young housewife from Vermont, won two gold medals in the slalom events in the 1952 Olympic Games. Billy Kidd and Jimmy Heuga won Olympic medals in the slalom twelve years later. In the 1980s, twin brothers Phil and Steve Mahre dominated American skiing and took home two Olympic medals. In 1994, Tommy Moe became the first American man to win two Olympic medals in a single Olympic competition.

Better Late Than Never

Alpine skiing was first dominated by Europeans, and U.S. skiers only slowly asserted their talents. After years of frustration, their diligence paid off at the 1964 Winter Olympics at Innsbruck, Austria, when Billy Kidd won a silver medal and teammate Jimmy Heuga won a bronze medal in the slalom. The Americans had finally left their tracks in the snow.

5

American Football

American football is an indoor or outdoor event in which two teams of eleven players each try to move a ball by running it on the ground or passing it through the air into the opponent's end zone. While it enjoys enormous popularity in the United States, it has failed to gather a strong following elsewhere in the world.

Equipment

The playing field in football is uniform through all levels, from grade school football to the professional ranks. The grass or synthetic turf stretches 100 yards (91.4 meters) long and 53.3 yards (48.8 meters) wide, with two additional 10-yard (9.14 meter) sections called *end zones*. The field is marked with a white out-of-bounds border on all four sides. Parallel white lines cross the field every five yards (4.57 meters), and large white numbers indicate the yard line every 10 yards. There are white hash marks along each sideline for each yard (.91 meters), and *goal lines* at each end of the playing field.

Goal posts sit on opposite out-of-bounds lines in each end zone. The gold or white metallic structures feature a horizontal crossbar 10 feet (3.05 meters) above the playing surface and posts, called *uprights*, 18.5 feet (5.6 meters) apart and 30 feet (9.14 meters) high. Field goal and kicked extra point attempts must pass through the goal posts to register points.

Players use an oval ball made from tan pebble grain approximately 11 inches (28 centimeters) long and 21.25 inches (54 centimeters) around at its broadest. It weighs around 14 ounces (396.9 grams).

Players wear uniforms and a helmet with a chin strap and face mask. Many players also wear protective gear, such as shoulder pads.

The Pass Is Born

One of the most revolutionary advances in football occurred in 1913 when two Notre Dame players introduced the forward pass to the game, which until then had relied solely on a running attack. Quarterback Gus Dorais completed thirteen passes that day to his end, Knute Rockne. Because of the new tactic, Notre Dame defeated a surprised Army squad 35-13, and changed the sport forever.

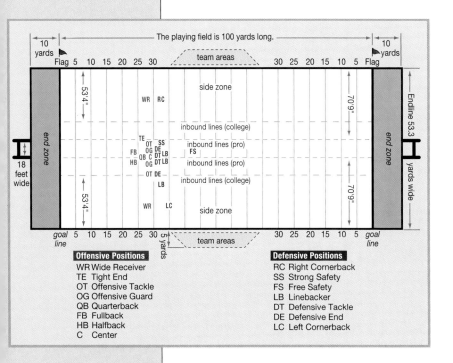

Offensive Positions
WR Wide Receiver
TE Tight End
OT Offensive Tackle
OG Offensive Guard
QB Quarterback
FB Fullback
HB Halfback
C Center

Defensive Positions
RC Right Cornerback
SS Strong Safety
FS Free Safety
LB Linebacker
DT Defensive Tackle
DE Defensive End
LC Left Cornerback

The Event

The team in possession of the ball puts its *offensive unit* on the field. The eleven players generally consist of five interior linemen (two *tackles*, two *guards*, and the *center*) who try to block their opponent, two *wide receivers* who either block or run downfield to catch passes, three backfield players (the *fullback*, the *halfback*, and the *tight end*) who run with the ball or head downfield for passes, and one *quarterback*, who controls the team. They attempt to move the ball steadily down the field and reach the end zone for a *touchdown*.

The *defensive unit* spreads its eleven players to guard the offensive players and put pressure on the quarterback. Their job is to prevent the offensive team from moving the ball downfield. The defensive unit may gain quick possession of the ball for its offensive unit by either recovering a fumble or intercepting a pass.

The offensive team may either run the football or throw passes. A play starts when the center *hikes* the ball (hands it back through his legs) to the quarterback. He can hand the ball to a running back, throw a pass to a receiver, or run with the ball himself. The team has four plays, called *downs*, to move 10 yards. If the team succeeds, it receives another four downs to move the next 10 yards. The offensive team continues to move the ball down the field until it either scores or is stopped by the defensive team. If, after three downs, the offensive team decides too many yards remain for it to cover in its final down, it *punts* (kicks) the ball to the other team.

Scoring is done in a variety of ways. A touchdown is worth six points. This occurs when a player advances the football into the opponent's end zone. A *field goal* occurs when the football is kicked over the crossbar and between the uprights. The team is awarded three points for a field goal. Two points are gained for a *safety*, which happens when an offensive player is tackled with the ball in his own end zone. An *extra-point* can be earned immediately following a touchdown by kicking the ball from the 3-yard line between the uprights. Two points are awarded if the ball is run or passed into the end zone.

Games are 60 minutes long and are divided into four 15-minute *quarters*. At the end of the second and fourth quarters, a 2-minute *warning* is called, which stops play. If the game is tied after regulation, a *sudden death* period is played. The first team to score wins the game. If the game is still tied after the 15-minute sudden death period, it is ruled a tie.

Dallas Cowboys quarterback Troy Aikman scrambles to elude New York Giants linebacker Lawrence Taylor.

History

American football originated from British rugby in the nineteenth century. In 1823 a soccer player from the Rugby School in England named William Webb Ellis picked up the ball during a soccer match and ran it across the goal line. Since this had never been done before, soccer purists condemned the move, while other players admired Ellis's actions. The game of rugby evolved from this incident. When both versions moved to the United States in the mid-1800s, a third form emerged, which led to American football.

The first intercollegiate football game occurred on November 6, 1869, in New Jersey, when Rutgers defeated Princeton 6–4. The next advancement occurred in 1874 in a game between Harvard and McGill University. In this

Joe Montana led the San Francisco 49ers to four Super Bowl championships.

contest, players were allowed to either kick, carry, or throw the ball. This style, which was for the first time called football, quickly spread throughout the eastern portions of the United States.

Walter Camp, called "the father of modern football," added structure to the game in the 1880s with new rules. He added the four-down feature and set the number of players at eleven per side. With these and other additions the college version prospered.

Professional football did not emerge as a force of its own until the 1920s. A league touting Jim Thorpe and the Chicago Bears's talented Red Grange took the field. In 1922 the league became the National Football League (NFL).

The National Football League gained popularity through the 1950s and 1960s, with players such as Jim Brown of the Cleveland Browns and Johnny Unitas of the Baltimore Colts setting records.

The American Football League, which appeared in 1960, merged with the NFL in 1970. The first Super Bowl was held in 1967, which pitted the NFL against the AFL. The Green Bay Packers defeated the Kansas City Chiefs 35-10. The Super Bowl has since grown into one of the nation's premier sporting events.

Hard Work Pays Off

Legendary Green Bay Packers head football coach Vince Lombardi earned a reputation for putting his players through rigorous practices. Though they grumbled and complained, in the end the men appreciated his system. Quarterback Bart Starr once explained, "Lombardi never accepted compromise, with himself or his players. He would drive us all week until there was nothing that could be unexpected, and the playing on Sunday would be the easiest part of the week."

Archery

Archery is the sport of shooting at targets with a bow and arrow. More than six million athletes perform in archery contests each year in the United States and Canada alone.

Equipment

Archers use one of three different types of bows—recurve, compound, and straight bow. The *recurve bow* has tips that curve away from the archer. A *compound bow* employs two cables and two to six pulleys so the bow is easier to draw. The *straight bow* is not used in competition as much anymore.

A bow's average length is 6 feet (1.8 meters) for men and 5.5 feet (1.7 meters) for women. Arrows range in length from 24 to 32 inches (61 to 81 centimeters) and consist of three main parts—the *point*, *shaft*, and *nock* (notch). Generally, the archer selects an arrow that is slightly longer than his or her arm.

The standard target for official competition is 48 inches (122 centimeters) in diameter, and stands 2 feet (61 centimeters) above the ground. An oilcloth or canvas face divides the target into five different bands—a gold bull's-eye 9.6 inches (24 centimeters) in diameter, followed by red, blue, black, and white bands each 4.8 inches (11 centimeters) wide.

The Event

Archery contests follow different formats. In target archery, contestants must hit circular targets from varying distances. In one competition, archers shoot thirty-six arrows at each of four different targets standing at 98 feet (30 meters), 164 feet (50 meters), 230 feet (70 meters), and 295 feet (90 meters).

Flight shooting is a competition for distance. Contestants either stand and shoot their

Quick-Draw Artists

Travelers in the American West in the years after the Civil War were stunned by the speed with which Native Americans could shoot arrows. George Catlin, the author of *Life Amongst the Indians* and other books, observed one Mandan fire a series of eight arrows before the first had hit the ground.

The archer pulls the bowstring back underneath her chin for optimum accuracy.

arrows, or lie on their backs and shoot with a bow that is strapped to their feet.

Field archery is similar to hunting. Competitors walk across a course and shoot at fourteen straw mats called butts. The butts vary in size and contain three circular scoring rings. Archers must shoot two rounds of four arrows each at targets set from 7 to 80 yards (6 to 72 meters) distant.

The ideal archery range consists of a level area of closely cropped grass in a reasonably sheltered position. There should be a safety zone of at least 25 yards (22.8 meters) behind the targets.

History

Archery began more than thirty thousand years ago when prehistoric hunting groups fashioned bows and arrows from wood and animal hides. Soldiers quickly adapted the hunting tool to a military weapon.

One of the most famous battles decided by archers was fought in 1415 at Agincourt, France between the English and the French. Led by King Henry V, 6,000 English archers so disrupted enemy ranks with their arrows that they turned back the numerically-superior French army of over thirty thousand men.

In the 1600s, King Charles II of England promoted archery as a sport, and in 1673 the first Ancient Scorton Arrow Contest, still conducted today, was held. The sport of archery first appeared in the United States in the 18th century, and was organized into an official activity in 1828 with the formation of the United Bowmen of Philadelphia. The National Archery Association conducted its first national tournament in 1879.

Australian Rules Football

Australian rules football is an indoor-outdoor sport in which two teams attempt to score points by putting the ball between posts set at opposite ends of the field. It is similar to American football, but it is still unique.

Equipment

The grass field is oval in shape and measures 120 to 170 yards (110 to 155 meters) wide and 150 to 200 yards (135 to 185 meters) long. The field is bounded by a white *boundary line*, and contains a *center circle* in the middle that is 10 feet (3 meters) in diameter.

Four posts stand at each end of the playing field. The *goal posts* consist of two posts at least 20 feet (6 meters) high and 21 feet (6.4 meters) apart. A white goal line runs from one post to the other. Two smaller posts, called *behind posts*, are set 21 feet behind the goal posts and are at least 10 feet (3 meters) high. White *behind lines* run from the goal posts to the behind posts. White *kickoff lines* are marked in front of the goal posts.

The oval ball measures 29.5 by 22.75 inches (736 by 572 millimeters) and weighs 16 ounces (454 grams). It has a rubber inside and a leather outside.

Players wear jerseys, shorts, socks, and shoes.

The Event

A game consists of four 25-minute quarters. Scoring is done in two ways. A *goal*, worth six points, is scored when one team puts the ball between the two goal posts. The ball must be kicked through the posts without any other player touching it. If it's touched,

Nathan Buckley

One of Australia's top talents is Nathan Buckley. The premier athlete astounds spectators with his long kicks and his skill at beating opponents to the ball. For his unselfish team play—he cares little about individual honors—and aggressive style, he was named team captain of the Collingwood Magpies. He has been a regular member of the All-Australia team during the 1990s.

Australian Rules Football is an exciting sport, but undoubtedly a sport of many bumps and bruises.

only one point is awarded. If the ball smacks off the goal post and does not go through the posts, only one point is given. A *behind*, worth 1 point, is scored when the ball passes between the goal posts and the behind posts.

Players advance the ball by either kicking it, running with it (as long as the player bounces the ball off the ground every 10 yards [9.14 meters]), or hand-passing it to a teammate. In this move, the athlete holds the ball in one hand and hits it with the clenched fist of the other hand. Throwing the ball is not permitted. Defending players may tackle the player with the ball or hold him. The player with the ball must then either kick or hand-pass the ball to a teammate to avoid a penalty.

History

Australian football started in 1858, when two Australian athletes modified a style of football played by Irish soldiers and miners working in the country. The game had few rules, so a wild, rough contest evolved. The first game occurred on August 7, 1858, when Scotch College met Melbourne Church of England Grammar School.

In its early years, Australian football contests sometimes lasted two or three days. At that time the game had no set time limit, but ended when one team scored two goals. The game's organizers realized this needed to be fixed, so in 1869 the rule was changed. The winner was whichever team had tallied the most points in a set time.

While Australian teams have toured other nations in an attempt to popularize their sport, they have met with limited success. Though a favorite on American television, it is not played in the United States.

Badminton

Badminton is a game in which two or four players hit a lightweight object, called a *shuttlecock*, back and forth over a net using thin rackets. It enjoyed an increase in popularity after World War II ended in 1945.

Date of Origin
1873
Place of Origin
England
Legendary Performers
Dr. David G. Freeman,
Judy Devlin Hashman
Governing Body
International Badminton
Association
Where They Compete
Worldwide
Championship Events
The Thomas Cup and the
Uber Cup competitions

Equipment

The regulation playing area measures 44 by 17 feet (13.4 by 5.2 meters) for singles and 3 feet (1 meter) wider for doubles. Rackets are thinner and lighter than in tennis. A shuttlecock is .18 ounces (5 grams) and made of cork and feathers. Players can enjoy the game almost anywhere outdoors or in gymnasiums.

The Event

A coin toss decides which side will serve first. That side will continue serving from alternate courts until it loses a rally. A player earns a point whenever the opponent fails to hit the shuttlecock over the net or hits the shuttlecock out of the playing area. The first side to reach either fifteen or twenty-one points, whichever is agreed to beforehand, wins.

China's Ge Fei takes a swat at the shuttlecock during the 1996 Summer Olympic Games.

Matches are best-of-three games played up to fifteen points. If competitors are playing just one game, the match extends to twenty-one points.

In singles play, the *server* hits diagonally across court (first from the right-hand side) to his opponent. If he wins the volley, he earns a point and serves again from the left-hand side of the court. If the opponent wins the volley, he then gains service. Only the player (or team) serving can score a point.

In doubles play, the two partners take turns serving. Only after both servers have been *downed*

14

(lost the volley following their serve) does the service go to the opposing team. So, in the doubles format, the receiving side must win two volleys before it gains service.

Service must be hit underhand. Players use either a *short service* or a *high service*. When using the short service, players attempt to serve a shot that barely soars over the net. This puts their opponent in a difficult position to hit their return shot. When using the high service, players hit the shuttlecock extremely high so it falls vertically. This also makes for a difficult shot for the opponent to handle.

There are four main strokes in badminton: the *clear*, the *smash*, the *drop*, and the *drive*. Each is hit with either a forehand or a backhand. The clear is sometimes called a lob or toss. It's hit high and aimed to land near the back *boundary line*. The smash is a reply to the clear. It's a forceful overhand shot struck from above the player's head. The drop is hit with a stiff wrist and barely falls over the net. The drive is a fast stroke (hit with a forehand or backhand) and is aimed to specific sides of the court. This shot is used when opposing players are caught out of position.

History

Badminton derives its name from the seat of the duke of Beaufort at Badminton in Gloucestershire. It developed around 1873 in Britain, an offshoot of an Indian game called *poona*. In 1893 the Badminton Association of England was formed. That body wrote the rules that govern the sport today.

Badminton quickly spread to Canada and the United States. The first badminton club in the United States was formed in New York City in 1878. The sport is governed in the United States by the American Badminton Association.

Baseball

Baseball is a team sport in which one side attempts to score more runs than the other. The game originated in the United States and is extremely popular in Japan, Central America, and South America.

Date of Origin
1845
Place of Origin
United States
Where They Compete
North and South America, Asia
Governing Body
Major League Baseball
Legendary Performers
Cy Young,
Ty Cobb,
Babe Ruth,
Ted Williams,
Willie Mays,
Hank Aaron,
Mark McGwire,
Ken Griffey, Jr.
Championship Event
World Series

Equipment

Baseball's playing field consists of an *infield* and an *outfield*. The infield has precise measurements, starting with its diamond shape. Each side of the diamond is 90 feet (27.4 meters) long and has either the *home plate* or a *base* at each corner.

The *pitcher's mound* is a domed circle of dirt culminating in a rectangular rubber slab called the *rubber*. The slab stands 60.5 feet (18 meters) from home plate. *Batter's boxes* designated by white chalk lines flank the left and right of home plate and indicate where the batter must stand. They measure 4 by 6 feet (1.2 by 1.8 meters).

The outfield refers to the plot of turf stretching from the infield to the fences. Outfields generally end anywhere from 310 to 450 feet (94 to 128 meters) from home plate.

White *foul lines* extend from home plate's apex to the outfield fence. They divide the playing field into *fair* and *foul territory*.

Players at bat use a circular wooden bat that is generally 34 inches (9 meters) long and 32 ounces (896 grams) in weight. They attempt to hit a *baseball* whose cork-and-rubber center is encased in tightly-woven woolen yarn. A leather casing is then stitched around the ball. It is 9 inches (22.9 centimeters) in circumference and weighs 5 ounces (141.7 grams). Fielders use leather gloves with which to catch the ball.

Players wear uniforms consisting of pants and jerseys with a team logo and a number (some teams also include the players' names). Spiked

Joltin' Joe

Joe DiMaggio of the New York Yankees set a record in 1941 that many believe will never be broken. Beginning on May 15, 1941, DiMaggio recorded a hit in fifty-six straight games. In that span he hit .408 and knocked in fifty-five runs.

16

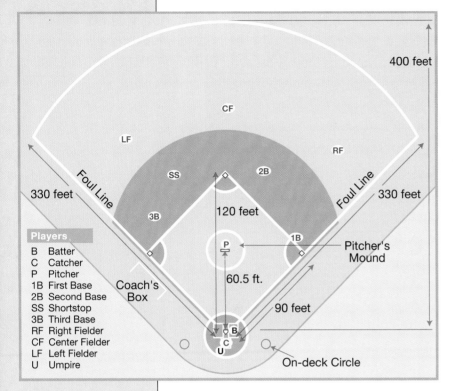

Players

B	Batter
C	Catcher
P	Pitcher
1B	First Base
2B	Second Base
SS	Shortstop
3B	Third Base
RF	Right Fielder
CF	Center Fielder
LF	Left Fielder
U	Umpire

shoes are worn over colored socks. All batters must wear a protective *helmet* with ear flaps.

The Event

A regulation baseball game lasts nine *innings*. Each team takes a turn at bat and in the field. The team at bat has three *outs* (batters or baserunners who do not reach base safely) each inning. An out can occur in many ways. The most common outs are when a batted ball is caught by a fielder before the ball touches the ground, when a baserunner is between bases and is touched by a fielder holding the ball, and when a batter strikes out. A strikeout occurs when the batter accumulates three strikes before four balls or hitting the ball. A run is scored each time a player successfully touches each of the four bases before the third out is registered.

The home team takes the field first. The *pitcher*, the player who throws balls to the opposing hitters, stands on the rubber on the pitcher's mound. The *catcher* squats behind home plate and catches any ball thrown by the pitcher that is not hit. Four players support the pitcher in the infield and three players take positions in the outfield.

The team at bat sends its players to bat in a set order determined by the team's *manager*. A player registers a *hit* when he bats the ball into fair territory and reaches a base safely. The batter may continue running to the next base, as long as he reaches it before a defensive player tags him with the ball in his glove.

If a batter hits a ball over the outfield fence, a *homerun* is called and the batter is allowed to touch all four bases and score a run. A batter may also reach base by being hit with a pitched ball, or if the other team makes an *error* (they drop the ball or bobble it).

The team at bat tries to score as many runs as possible before the third out. The team with the highest run total after nine innings wins the contest. If the teams are tied, extra innings are added until one outscores the other.

The most important player on the field is the pitcher. His performance is the most influential to his team's success. A pitcher is credited with the win if his team wins, and the loss if his team loses. He can also achieve great individual accomplishments in a game. He can throw a *shutout* (no runs scored against him the entire game), a *no-hitter* (no hits against him the entire game), or a *perfect game* (no runs, hits, walks, or errors the entire game).

History

Baseball can be traced as far back as the Middle Ages, when athletes played a game called stoolball. In 1845, Alexander Cartwright of New York devised a set of rules for the game. Modern baseball was born.

The first game was played on June 19, 1846. The New York Nine defeated the Knickerbockers 23-1 in four innings.

After the Civil War ended in 1865, baseball teams appeared in many large cities. When Alfred James Reach signed a contract to play for a Philadelphia team, professional baseball was born. The National League was formed in 1876, and the American League started in 1901. Two years later the first World Series

Toronto Blue Jays pitcher David Wells sets his eyes on the target early in his delivery.

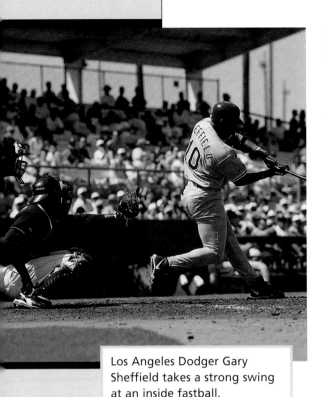

Los Angeles Dodger Gary Sheffield takes a strong swing at an inside fastball.

pitted the top teams in each league against each other.

Baseball's popularity soared in the 1920s with the arrival of George Herman "Babe Ruth." It's still referred to as America's national pastime. The New York Yankees have the largest fan base of any team in organized sports. Their popularity is not a surprise. In the twentieth century, the Yankees won twenty-five World Series championships. In 1998, Mark McGwire and Sammy Sosa captured the world's attention and renewed interest in baseball with their incredible chase of Roger Maris's single-season homerun record. McGwire set a new record with 70 homers, while Sosa hit 66.

Best of the Best

A popular debate among baseball fans concerns the greatest players of all time. Many will name Babe Ruth as the best, but others will argue for names like Ty Cobb, Roger Hornsby, Willie Mays, Lou Gehrig, Ted Williams, Joe DiMaggio, Mickey Mantle, Hank Aaron, and Ken Griffey, Jr. At the 1999 All-Star Game, the top 100 players of the century were selected. Ruth was the top vote-getter and named the greatest baseball player of the twentieth century.

Negro Leagues

For many years major league baseball excluded African Americans from participating. In response, separate Negro leagues showcased the talents of fabulous athletes. Pitcher Leroy "Satchel" Paige baffled hitters well into his forties, and homerun hitter Josh Gibson has been called by many observers the best player in the game. These men prepared the way for future African American players to enter the major leagues. The first to do so was Jackie Robinson in 1947.

Basketball

Basketball is a sport where two teams of five attempt to throw a round ball through a 10-foot high hoop. It originated in the United States and is now popular worldwide.

Equipment

Basketball is played on courts measuring 50 feet (15.24 meters) wide and 94 feet (28.65 meters) long. Indoor courts feature hardwood floors, while their outdoor counterparts are made of concrete or asphalt.

Metal rim *baskets* 18 inches (45 centimeters) in diameter rest at opposite ends of the court. Also called the *hoop*, the basket stands 10 feet (3.05 meters) above the floor and supports a white cord *net*. The *rim* is attached to a flat *backboard* measuring 6 by 4 feet (1.8 by 1.2 meters).

A *division line* cuts the court into two equal sections. Two center circles indicate the spot where the game's opening tip-off occurs. *Free throw lines* at each end mark where a player shoots free throws. The free throw line rests 15 feet (4.57 meters) from the backboard, and any player shooting a free throw must stand behind that line.

The *three-point field goal line* stretches in a semicircle in front of each basket. If a player shoots the basketball through the hoop from behind this line, he or she receives three points. In the professional game, the line is 23 feet 9 inches (7.02 meters) from the basket.

The *basketball* has a circumference of 30 inches (78 centimeters) and weighs about 22 ounces (624 grams). It consists of a rough leather, rubber, or synthetic cover. Players dress in shorts, socks, leather basketball shoes, wrist bands, and jerseys with numbers on the front and back.

Wilt the Stilt

Wilt Chamberlain attained heights in scoring that no one has ever approached. During the 1961–62 season, Chamberlain set a record by averaging 50.4 points per game. On March 2, 1962, of that season, he scored an astounding one hundred points against the New York Knicks.

20

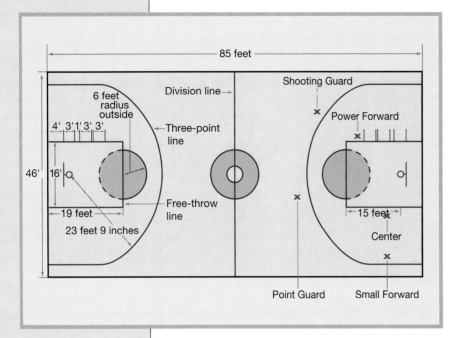

Diagram labels:
- 85 feet
- Division line →
- Shooting Guard
- 6 feet radius outside
- 4' 3'1'3' 3'
- ← Three-point line
- Power Forward
- 46' 16'
- Free-throw line
- 19 feet
- ← 15 feet →
- 23 feet 9 inches
- Center
- Point Guard
- Small Forward

The Event

The game begins with both teams lining up around the center circle for the opening *jump ball*, or *tip-off*. One player from each side stands inside the center circle, while the other eight players stand to the outside. The referee tosses the ball into the air, and both players try to tip it to a teammate. The team that wins possession of the ball then tries to move it into the opponent's area for a basket.

The teams of five players have two guards, two forwards, and one center. Generally speaking, the center and forwards are taller than the guards. Players advance the ball by *dribbling*—bouncing it on the ground with one hand—or by passing it to a teammate. The object is to shoot the ball through the hoop.

The opposing five players try to defend their basket by intercepting passes, blocking shots, or grabbing the rebound of a missed shot. They then attempt to advance the ball to the other end of the court to make a basket.

Two points are awarded for a field goal. This occurs when a shot passes through the hoop while the ball is in play. Three points are given for any shot made from outside the three-point line. One point is handed out to each successful free throw.

A player receives a free throw whenever he or she is fouled by the other team. Examples of fouls are: holding a player, hitting an opponent, and pushing from behind.

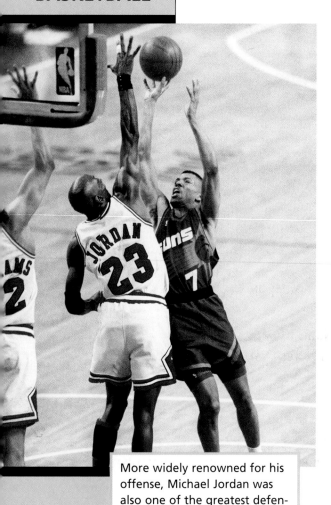

More widely renowned for his offense, Michael Jordan was also one of the greatest defensive players of his time.

After a basket is made, the ball is given to the opposing team. Play continues until a foul is committed, the ball goes out of bounds, or a time out is called. Professional contests consist of four twelve-minute quarters, while college games last two twenty-minute halves. The team with the most points at game's end is the winner.

History

Dr. James A. Naismith invented the game that is played today. Naismith formulated the game in 1891 as a solution to there not being enough sporting events offered in winter. He wanted to create a game that could be played indoors. The first intercollegiate game occurred in 1897. One year later, the first professional league was started.

In 1934, colleges made the first big impact on basketball. A sportswriter named Ned Irish convinced promoters at New York's Madison Square Garden to schedule doubleheaders between college teams. The first—between Notre Dame, New York University, Westminster, and St. John's— drew enthusiastic crowds. Four years later the Garden hosted the first National Invitational Tournament.

After a slow start, professional basketball emerged as a strong contender for spectator interest when two leagues merged in 1949 to form the National Basketball Association (NBA). The Boston Celtics, led by Bill Russell and Bob Cousy, dominated the league in the 1960s by capturing eleven titles in thirteen years.

In the 1970s and early 1980s, women's leagues were organized, but suffered from low attendance. However, the Women's National

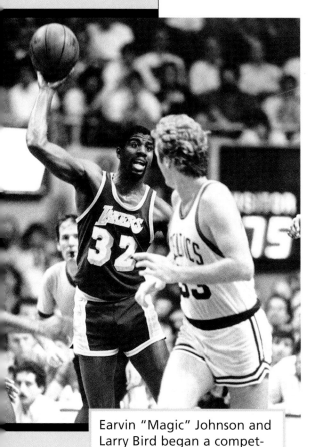

Earvin "Magic" Johnson and Larry Bird began a competitive rivalry in college that continued throughout their NBA careers.

Basketball Association (WNBA), conceived in 1996, has developed a strong spectator interest. The Houston Comets, led by Cynthia Cooper, won three straight WNBA titles.

Best of the Best

Though the NBA is only a little more than fifty years old, it's had its share of stars on the court. Wilt Chamberlain revolutionized the center position, and dominated league play throughout most of his career in the 1960s and 70s. His nemesis, Bill Russell, proved that success can be earned by playing intimidating defense. Names like Oscar Robertson, Elgin Baylor, Jerry West, and Walt Frazier also had a major impact on the way the game was played.

In the 1970s, Julius Erving brought a new style of play to the game. His high-flying acrobatics brought the game above the rim. Magic Johnson, Larry Bird, Michael Jordan, and Patrick Ewing were catalysts during the 1980s in helping the NBA grow in popularity.

Since the retirement of basketball legend Michael Jordan, several young players have emerged. Grant Hill, Kobe Bryant, and Tim Duncan are just a few athletes who are tops in the game today.

Shooting Star

Kobe Bryant of the Los Angeles Lakers entered the draft directly out of high school in 1996. This flashy and competitive player has been compared to Michael Jordan. In only his fourth season in the NBA, Bryant helped guide the Lakers to an NBA championship in 2000, defeating the Indiana Pacers. If he wants to match Jordan in championship rings, however, he still has five more to go.

Billiards

Billiards is played on a rectangular, felt-covered table. The player uses a *cue stick* to hit *cue balls* into pockets. The three most common forms of billiards are *pocket billiards*, *carom billiards*, and *snooker*. The game is popular in many countries.

Equipment

The table has a slate surface called a *bed*. It is covered with felt to give a smooth roll for the balls. The playing surface is surrounded by a rubber cushion, or *rail*. Though tables vary in size, they are twice as long as they are wide. Pocket billiard and snooker tables have six pockets into which the pool balls are hit. Carom billiards tables do not have pockets.

Wooden cue sticks are between 53 and 60 inches (134 to 152 centimeters) in length and end in a leather tip. The pool balls are made of hard plastic.

The Event

Pocket billiards uses fifteen differently colored balls numbered one through fifteen, plus a white cue ball that the player hits with the cue stick. Play begins with the fifteen balls *racked* (arranged) in triangular fashion at one end of the table. In the *break*, the player hits the cue ball at the triangle from anywhere behind an imaginary line at the table's opposite end.

The most popular form of competitive pocket billiards in the United States is straight pool. After the break, the players try to make a continuous run of balls until only one remains. The other fourteen are then racked with a space left at the head. The player who sank the fourteenth ball now tries to sink the fifteenth, and break the new stack at the same time. Each player shoots until a miss; then the next player shoots. One point is awarded for each ball sunk, and the game continues

Legendary billiards player Minnesota Fats was a billiards wizard who could shoot pool with either hand.

until one contestant reaches 150 points. The winner stays on the table while the next contestant racks the balls.

Carom billiards uses two white balls as cue balls for the players, and one red ball. There are no pockets on the table in carom billiards. The players try to hit the cue ball at one of the other two balls, then have it hit three cushions before hitting a second ball. Snooker uses twenty-one balls of varying colors. The player must sink a red ball, then a different colored ball, then a red, and so on. Each color represents a different point total.

In any shot but a break shot, a player's cue ball may contact either of the object balls first. A player's turn continues until he or she fails to score.

Among casual players, *8-ball* is most prevalent. After the break, one player attempts to sink all balls numbered one through seven, while the other targets balls numbered nine through fifteen. After sinking seven designated balls, the player tries to make the 8-ball, at which time the game ends.

A tournament contestant takes his shot in a pool hall in Beijing, China.

History

The word billiards comes from the French word *bille*, meaning small ball. The game started in England in the fourteenth century, and came to the American continent in the 1500s. Some of the greatest players in the United States were Jacob Schaefer, Sr., Willie Hoppe, and Willie Mosconi.

Multi-talented

Wolfgang Amadeus Mozart was apparently talented in more than just music. A close friend wrote in his diary that the famed composer of countless musical classics performed almost as well on the billiards table. The associate stated Mozart "was fond of billiards and had an excellent table in his home. Many and many a game have I played with him, but always came off second best."

25

Bobsled Racing

Bobsledding, or bobsleighing, is a race where a team of two or four bobsledders navigate a steep, icy path in specially-designed sleds. The sport is especially popular in Europe and North America.

Equipment

The riding surface of the steel, aluminum, or fiberglass sled reaches about 11 feet (3.3 meters) in length for four-person teams and 9 feet (2.7 meters) for two-person squads. It is attached to two supporting sleds, each resting on metal runners. The front sled is steered by the front man with either a wheel or rope. The back sled supports the two- or four-person units. The back sled also contains the brake, a bar made of hardened steel with serrated edges for cutting into the ice.

A bobsled course consists of snow and ice packed down to create a lightning-quick track. High banks of ice and snow tower along both sides to keep the bobsled on course. Sleds can attain speeds of up to 90 miles (145 kilometers) per hour.

Members of the East German bobsled team push the sled to build momentum before it reaches the starting line.

The Event

The front person, called the *skipper*, steers the bobsled while the last sledder, called the *brakeman*, stops the bobsled. He also prevents the sled from skidding out of control. In four-person teams, the extra two people add weight to help control the sled. By carefully shifting their weight from one side to the other, the two extra people help guide the sled down the run.

The race starts with the team members grabbing the sled about 49 feet (15 meters) behind the starting line. They run and push the sled from behind or alongside to build

The front man (skipper) steers the bobsled while the rear man (brakeman) controls the brake to avoid skidding out of control.

momentum. The men jump into the sled as it approaches the starting line, then duck down as the sled whisks along the course.

Intimate knowledge of the course is very important to the racing team. If the sled even touches the steep, packed ice banking, the team will likely lose a vital split second.

History

Bobsledding originated in St. Moritz, Switzerland in 1888. A group of American and English tourists, disenchanted with the lack of thrills offered by Swiss tobogganing, connected two sleighs with a board. Ten years later, the first organized competition occurred in the same Swiss city. In 1902, St. Moritz became the home of the first specially-built bobsled run.

Though the event appeared in the 1924 Olympic Games and remains a feature of the Winter Olympics, bobsledding has not developed the huge following enjoyed by many other activities because of its danger. The International Bobsled Federation supervises international competitions.

The most renowned bobsledder in the sport's history is Italy's Eugenio Monti. He piloted eleven crews to world championships from 1957 to 1968. In the United States, Billy Fiske won two Olympic gold medals. In his honor, each year the Billy Fiske Memorial Trophy is awarded to the top American amateur bobsled team.

Olympic Harmony

The first African Americans to participate for the United States in the Winter Olympics did so during the 1980 games at Lake Placid, New York. Willie Davenport, who had won a gold medal in the 110-meter high hurdle event in the 1968 Summer Olympics, teamed with Jeff Gadley and two other athletes to compete in the four-man bobsled event. Unhappily, they finished a distant twelfth.

Boccie

Boccie is a form of bowling that developed, in its modern form, in Italy. It is popular in that nation, as well as in the United States, Australia, and South America.

Date of Origin
Approximately 5200 B.C.
Place of Origin
Italy
Legendary Performer
Rico Daniele,
Phil Ferari
Governing Body
United States
Boccie Federation
Where They Compete
Italy,
United States,
Australia,
South America
Championship Events
World Series of Boccie,
Superball Classic

Equipment

Boccie balls are made of wood or a synthetic material. Athletes toss or roll larger balls that are 4.5 inches (11 centimeters) in diameter at a smaller *target ball* that is 2.75 inches (7 centimeters) in diameter. The larger balls weigh a little over 2 pounds (906 grams). The target ball is also called a *pallino* or *jack*.

Athletes perform on a smooth playing surface. A standard field is 91 feet (27 meters) long and 13 feet (3.9 meters) wide. Three lines divide the playing area—a *center line* extends across the field's mid-section, while a *foot line* runs across the court 15 feet (4.5 meters) in from the opposite ends. *Backboards*, which are side and back walls 10 inches (.25 meters) high, enclose the entire playing field.

The Event

Games are played by teams of two or four members, half of whom are stationed at each end of the court. The winner of the coin flip decides whether to toss the pallino to the other end or to choose at which end play begins. The first player has two chances to toss the pallino beyond the court's center line. Should he or she fail, the other team receives two chances.

When the pallino has been properly rolled, a player throws the first boccie ball toward it. The other side then rolls its initial ball. If it rests inside the first ball, they stop rolling and the opponent returns. If its ball does not stop closer to the pallino, that team continues until either it places a ball closer to the

Four balls in play surround the small orange ball, called a pallino.

pallino, or it rolls all four balls. The players may elect to use their ball to deflect an opponent's ball farther from the pallino if they wish. The competitors complete a frame when both teams have rolled all four balls.

If a player's foot steps on or beyond the foot line, or if the ball hits the backboard, the ball is declared "dead."

Points are given for the balls resting closest to the pallino. A team receives one point for each ball that sits nearer the pallino than the opponent's closest one. After the completed frame, the team that scored points tosses the target ball back down to the court's other end. The first team to compile twelve points wins the game.

When a team wins a game, players exchange ends of the court and substitutions may be made. The winning team tosses the pallino to start the next game.

Baseball great Joe DiMaggio tries his hand at boccie.

History

The first evidence of boccie was found in the grave of an ancient Egyptian dating to about 5200 B.C. Sculptures and paintings from ancient Greece and Rome show men involved in activities similar to boccie.

A Brain Game

To be played properly, boccie requires competitors to think about their rolls. Rather than trying to place the ball closer to the pallino, it might be advantageous to either knock an opponent's ball farther away, nudge one of one's own closer, or place one of one's own in front of the pallino or in front of one's own ball to prevent the other team from deflecting it.

As the game was imported to other countries, variations of boccie developed. Lawn bowls flourished in England and Scotland, while skittles became popular in France and England. Boccie was warmly embraced in Italy. The game built a loyal following in the United States when Italian immigrants arrived in the late 1800s. The game is mostly enjoyed at family gatherings, barbecues, and other outdoor activities.

Bowling

Bowling is a sport in which one attempts to knock down ten bottle-shaped maple *pins* by rolling a hard ball across a smooth surface. It is most popular in the United States.

Equipment

A *bowling ball* is made from hard rubber or another non-metallic substance. It has two or three finger holes the bowler uses to grasp the object. The ball may not be larger than 27 inches (69 centimeters) around or weigh more than 16 pounds (7.2 kilograms).

The lane, or *alley*, is 42 inches (106 centimeters) wide and 62 feet 10.18 inches (19.15 meters) long from the *foul line* to the *pit*, where the pins are. A *gutter*, a shallow depression running along either side of the alley, catches any ball that veers off the alley.

The hard maple pins weigh between 2 pounds 14 ounces (1.3 kilograms) and 3 pounds 10 ounces (1.6 kilograms). Four rows of pins are arranged in triangular fashion, with the *headpin* standing alone. Machinery automatically resets the pins after each frame.

The Event

The bowler advances along an approach of 15 feet (4.5 meters) and must release the ball before reaching the foul line. The competitor gets two rolls for each *frame*. If all ten pins are knocked down with the first roll, it's called a *strike*—this gives the bowler ten points plus the total number of pins knocked down on the next two rolls. If any pins remain standing after the first roll, the bowler rolls a second ball at the remainder in hopes of knocking them over. If all the remaining pins are knocked down, the bowler receives a *spare*—ten points plus the total number of pins knocked down on the next roll. If any pins remain standing after the

Athletes participating in the 33rd Bowling World Cup traveled to the deserts of Cairo, Egypt, to compete.

second roll, the bowler receives only points for the number of pins knocked down in that frame.

History

Some form of bowling appears in most ancient cultures. Archaeologists unearthed five-thousand-year-old bowling balls and pins from the grave of an Egyptian child. In the fourth century, Germans rolled large stones at balanced clubs in a religious ceremony. The clubs represented evil. This practice spread throughout Europe and into England, where the world's first indoor bowling lane opened in 1445.

The Dutch brought bowling with them to North America in the 1600s. In 1732 New York City residents established an area that was used for bowling, and this same section is known today as Bowling Green.

Nine pins, a variation of modern bowling in which nine pins are arranged in diamond fashion, was popular in the United States in the 1800s. However, anti-gambling influences led to several states banning the game.

In 1895 the American Bowling Congress formulated rules for the game. The Congress sponsors annual national bowling tournaments in singles, doubles, and five-person team competitions. It is still the official governing body in many nations.

In 1952, the introduction of automatic pinsetters quickened the pace of the game. Bigger bowling centers were constructed, and families began to enjoy the game together.

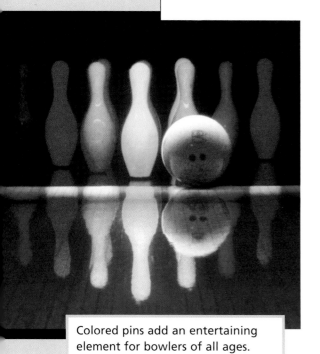

Colored pins add an entertaining element for bowlers of all ages.

Top Talents

Bowling produced a list of quality athletes in the 1950s and 1960s, but the two finest were Don Carter, on the men's side, and Marion Ladewig, on the women's side. Carter was named Bowler of the Year six times between 1953 and 1962 and helped popularize the game with television audiences. Starting in 1950, Ladewig, a grandmother from Michigan, was named Bowler of the Year ten times in fourteen years.

31

Boxing

Boxing, which has been called the "manly art of self-defense," is a sport in which two contestants try to hit each other with gloved fists. The object is to either knock out the opponent or to dominate the match and win on points.

Equipment

Boxing matches occur in a *ring*. It measures from 16 to 20 square feet (4.9 to 6 meters) for amateur bouts and from 16 to 24 square feet (4.9 to 7.3 meters) for professional contests. Boxers wear padded leather gloves, trunks, and lightweight shoes.

The Event

Each *round* of a match lasts three minutes, with a one-minute interval between rounds. Amateur bouts last either three or five rounds, while professional fights range from four to fifteen rounds.

A match may be won in three different ways: A boxer succeeds in knocking his opponent to the canvas with such force that he or she can't rise within ten seconds; the referee stops the match because one of the boxers cannot safely continue; or judges award more points to the boxer who dominated the match. In the event that neither boxer wins on points, a draw (tie) is declared.

Boxers may not hit below the belt, kick, trip, or strike an opponent who is down or on one knee. Too many fouls—or one very serious foul—may result in victory being awarded to the other fighter.

Both professional and amateur boxing has different weight classes into which the athletes are placed. These classes range from under 106 pounds in the strawweight class to over 190 pounds in the heavyweight class.

Date of Origin
1700s
Place of Origin
England
Legendary Performers
John L. Sullivan,
Joe Louis,
Rocky Marciano,
Muhammad Ali,
Sugar Ray Leonard,
Evander Holyfield
Governing Bodies
U.S. Amateur
Boxing Federation,
World Boxing Association,
World Boxing Council,
International Boxing
Federation
Where They Compete
Worldwide
Championship Events
Olympic Games,
Title bouts in different
weight divisions

Muhammad Ali referred to himself as "the greatest of all time." Few could argue.

History

Evander Holyfield knocks down challenger Michael Moorer in a heavyweight title bout.

The Greeks believed that the gods participated in boxing on Mount Olympus, and they included the sport in the Olympic Games around 688 B.C. After the Romans conquered Greece, they adapted boxing for their gladiators.

James Figg, a famous English athlete, introduced modern boxing in the early 1700s. Figg practiced and taught the *bare-knuckle* (gloveless) style of fighting. James Broughton, another noted fighter, introduced rules in 1743 that eventually governed the sport.

Boxing took hold in the United States in the 1880s, when John L. Sullivan, a superb American bare-fisted boxer, toured the nation to stage gloved boxing exhibitions. It gradually spread throughout the U.S. and enjoyed its "golden age" in the 1920s and 1930s. Fighters such as Jack Dempsey and Joe Louis delighted audiences for years.

Queensbury Rules

These rules, compiled in the 1860s, provide the foundation for modern boxing. Among the twelve rules is a clause banning wrestling, another stating that a boxer knocked to the canvas has ten seconds to rise unassisted or lose the bout, a rule requiring the boxers to wear gloves, and a regulation setting the round's duration at three minutes. Boxers ever since have adhered to these landmark regulations.

During the 1960s and 1970s, Muhammad Ali dominated the sport. Other notables, such as Joe Frazier, George Foreman, and Larry Holmes also left their mark in the ring. Ali, Foreman, and Frazier each held the heavyweight title belt during the 1970s. Ali won the title three times during his career. Holmes was the heavyweight champ from 1978 to 1985.

Since then, boxing has lacked a dominant champion. Mike Tyson, Evander Holyfield, Riddick Bowe, Lennox Lewis, and even Foreman, coming out of retirement, have each held the distinction of heavyweight champion.

Bullfighting

Bullfighting pits a bullfighter, called the *matador*, against a specially-bred bull. The matador and his or her assistants entice the bull into charging, until the matador ends the spectacle by plunging a sword between the animal's shoulders. The event is Spain's national sport and is popular in Mexico, Portugal, southern France, and much of Latin America.

Equipment

The matador wears brightly-colored clothes for the event. The tight knee-length pants and a short jacket are richly embroidered with gold and silver. A winged black hat covers the matador's distinctive hair-style, which features a long braid hanging down the back of his or her neck. The matador must control the animal's behavior in the ring and perform with grace and style. In the contest, people on foot, called *banderilleros*, and on horseback, called *picadores*, assist the matador.

Cristina Sánchez executes a chest pass during a bullfight in Segovia, Spain.

The bull, specially bred for the fight, must be three to four years old, weigh over 1,000 pounds (450 kilograms), have no physical defects, and be aggressive and strong. The fight occurs in a *bullring*, or *plaza de toros*. The circular arena extends 55 yards (50 meters) in diameter and has a surface of packed sand.

The Event

There are two main types of bullfights. The *corrida de toros* features the most respected matadors, called *matadores de toros*, who receive the special title based on previous exploits. In the other type, less skilled matadors, called *novilleros*, fight the bull. In both events, three matadors each fight two bulls, one at a time. The typical bullfight begins when a trumpeter's blast announces the entry of riders on horseback, called *alguaciles*.

They ride across the ring to an official's box and receive the key to open the *toril* (stall), where the bulls are stored.

At the sound of a second trumpet blast, the bull emerges from the toril. Three banderilleros take turns waving a cape to make the bull charge.

A third trumpet sound brings the two picadores, who thrust long lances into the bull's neck to weaken its muscles. A final trumpet brings the matador with sword and cape. After teasing the bull into charges, the matador plunges a sword into a small spot between the bull's shoulders. If accurate, the bull dies almost instantly.

Depending upon his or her performance, the matador then circles the arena to loud acclaim. The dignitary may present him or her with one of the bull's ears as a trophy. For exceptional performances, the matador may receive both ears, or even the ears and tail.

History

Bullfighting originated with the ancient Minoans of Crete. Specially-trained youths grabbed the horns of charging bulls and somersaulted over their backs. Julius Caesar entertained Roman audiences by importing bullfights from the Iberian Peninsula (modern Spain and Portugal).

When Muslims from Africa, called Moors, conquered Spain in A.D. 711, they transformed bullfighting by including horses and lances. The next advance occurred in 1725 when Francisco Romero used a sword and fought on foot. Other notable matadors include Manolete, gored to death in 1947, and Manuel Benitez, called El Cordobes. Bullfighting is still a popular event in Spain today.

Manolete

Few modern matadors have been so revered as Manuel Rodriguez, known as Manolete, whose graceful motions and fearlessness in the ring astounded crowds. However, during a bullfight in August 1947, a bull gored Manolete in his right thigh. As a stunned crowd watched silently, Manolete was taken to the infirmary, but bled to death that afternoon. Spain reveres Manolete's memory each year on the anniversary of his death.

Canadian Football

Canadian rules football is very similar to the version played in the United States. It is a game played by two teams of twelve players each who attempt to move the football downfield for a score.

Equipment

At 110 yards (100.58 meters) long and 65 yards (59.44 meters) wide, the field is larger than that used in the United States. It has much deeper end zones, which extend 25 yards (22.86 meters) from the goal line instead of the American 10 yards (9.14 meters). Every 5 yards (4.57 meters) white *chalk lines* run across the field parallel to the goal lines. *Goal posts* stand on each *goal line* and must be at least 20 feet (6 meters) tall and 18.5 feet (5.6 meters) apart, joined by a crossbar.

Players use a leather-like oval ball approximately 11 inches (28 centimeters) long and 21.25 inches (54 centimeters) around at its broadest. It weighs about 14 ounces (396.9 grams).

The Event

The team on offense receives three downs to move the ball 10 yards. If they succeed, they receive another three downs. If they fail, the other team gains possession. Canadian football has one less down than American football and allows twelve players on the field. This forces the Canadian game to feature a more wide-open, aggressive style of offense.

The offensive team scores a *touchdown* worth six points when it pushes the ball into its opponent's end zone. It adds one point for a successful conversion kick from the 5-yard line following the touchdown, or two points for running or throwing

Doug Flutie became a superstar in the Canadian Football League before returning to the NFL.

the ball into the end zone. Teams also gain three points through *field goals*, which are kicks anywhere from the field that pass through the goal post uprights. A team receives two points for a *safety*, which is tackling the opponent carrying the ball in his own end zone. A *rouge*, which occurs when a ball is kicked into the opponent's end zone and the opponent fails to advance the ball out to the field of play, is worth one point.

History

Canadian football is an outgrowth of rugby. While playing similar games for much of the late 1800s, it began diverging from American football as the 1900s dawned. In 1891 the Canadian Rugby Union was organized. Sixteen years later a four-team league (Hamilton, Toronto, Montreal, Ottawa) was formed and is called the Canadian Football League today.

The governor general of Canada, Albert Henry George, the fourth earl Grey, donated a trophy in 1909. It was to be given each year to the top team. From that humble beginning, the Grey Cup competition has evolved into Canada's version of the Super Bowl.

Each team may only include fourteen American athletes on its squad of thirty-two players. The rest must be Canadian citizens. League officials hoped to gradually build the game into a strong Canadian sport and give its own athletes greater opportunities to excel.

While such American athletes as Joe Theisman and Doug Flutie starred in Canadian football, their accomplishments have been equaled or surpassed by Canadian stars. Russ Jackson, quarterback for the Ottawa Rough Riders for twelve years, was voted the outstanding player in the Canadian Football League three times in the 1960s.

A Wide Open Game

Besides a larger playing field and an extra player on offense and defense, Canadian football features other differences from American football. Offensive backs may be in forward motion before the ball is put into play, defensive players must remain at least one yard away from the offensive line, and punts that roll into the end zone must be run out.

Canoe Sailing

Canoe sailing is a specific type of race that dates back to the 1860s. The purpose is to complete a specific course in the shortest time. It is also a recreational sport enjoyed around the world.

Equipment

The most common canoe used for sailing is called the Class C rig. The canoe is about 18 feet (5.4 meters) long and about 3 feet (.9 meters) wide. Since the canoe is usually handled by one person, the Class C rig's sail can be easily lowered in strong winds.

The canoe features a wooden or aluminum *mast* and vertical *spars*, (frames used to support the sail). Three lines—the *halyard*, the *sheet*, and the *boom vang*—stretch from the canoe to different parts of the mast and rigging and help stabilize the canoe. The halyard raises and lowers the sail, the sheet maintains control of the sail in heavy winds, and the boom vang prevents the boom (the spar supporting the lower part of the sail) from lifting in strong winds. The canoeist also uses a rudder for steering.

The Event

The American Canoe Association sponsors canoe sailing in the United States. While six classes of sailing canoes exist, normally only three are used in competition. The three most frequently used are the cruising class canoe, which is rudderless and thus must be steered by shifting weight or with a paddle; the popular C class canoe; and the decked sailing canoe, generally used in international sailing events.

The cruising class canoe is used in the Olympic Games and now has 16 events. The events are divided into two sections—*flatwater* and *whitewater slalom*. The designs of the boats are a bit different for the two different venues.

Olympic competitor Michal Matikan of Slovakia battles the elements during the slalom canoe event.

The flatwater boats are built long and thin to enhance hull speed. The whitewater boats are built shorter and stockier for better maneuverability and to prevent water intake.

Flatwater races require speed from start to finish. Each canoe must stay in its own *lane*, which is 30 feet (9 meters) wide. It must stay at least 16 feet (5 meters) away from its competing neighbor. If a canoe comes too close to an opponent, it is disqualified. The first contestant to cross the finish line wins the race.

The whitewater events take place in rapidly moving water. Races range from 440 to 1,320 yards (400 to 1,200 meters) in length. The courses are man-made to create whitewater conditions found in the wilderness. The winner of the race is the competitor who runs the course the fastest. A two-second penalty is added to a time if the competitor touches a gate, and a fifty-second penalty is added if a gate is missed.

Elite-level canoe athletes have the characteristics of a well-defined body builder and a lean marathon runner. It takes years of training for a paddler to become internationally competitive. The average athlete at the elite level is in his or her mid-twenties.

The History

John MacGregor

No one was more responsible for popularizing canoeing than John MacGregor. In addition to building the first Rob Roy double-paddle canoe, he wrote bestselling books and articles about his adventures and delivered lectures to eager audiences. His book *A Thousand Miles in the Rob Roy on the Lakes and Rivers of Europe* helped bring the sport to thousands of enthusiasts.

Organized sport canoeing started with England's Royal Canoe Club in 1866, founded by Scottish adventurer John MacGregor.

The club held its first regatta the following year, and boasted more than 300 enthusiasts by 1868. The sport's popularity spread throughout Europe and North America. The New York Canoe Club was founded in 1871. After years of frustration, canoeing was finally added as a full medal sport for the 1936 Olympic Games held in Berlin.

Court Handball

Handball is a game played on an indoor court by two players (singles) or four players (doubles). A small rubber ball is struck with the hands against either a single wall or the four walls of an enclosed court.

Date of Origin	**1200s**
Place of Origin	**Ireland**
Legendary Performers	**Phil Casey, Joe Platak**
Governing Body	**The U.S. Handball Association**
Where They Compete	**Worldwide**
Championship Event	**Four-Wall National Championship**

Equipment

Handball players wear padded leather gloves on each hand. Gloves must be light in color, and may not be webbed, connected, or removed. Competitors smack a hard rubber ball that is 1.875 inches (4.8 centimeters) in diameter. The most common handball court is the enclosed four-wall court. It measures 20 feet (6 meters) wide and 40 feet (12 meters) long. A 20-foot (6 meters) high *front wall* is connected to the 14-foot (4.3 meters) high rear wall by the *side walls*.

White lines mark different zones on the court. A short line runs across the court's middle, and the service line runs 5 feet (1.5 meters) in front. The *server* must stand between these two lines. In doubles his partner stands to the side in an area called the *service box*.

The Event

The server stands in the service area, bounces the handball and hits it with one hand against the front wall. The ball must land between the short line and the back wall before hitting any other wall. If the ball fails to go beyond the short line, the player serves again. If that attempt also fails, the opponent gets to serve.

The opponent returns the ball by hitting it before it bounces twice on the floor. The

Court handball can be played in-doors or outdoors by athletes of all ages.

In four-wall handball players must frequently turn their back to the front wall to find the ball and strike it.

players may bounce the ball against any of the four walls, as long as it strikes the front wall before hitting the floor. Players or teams alternate hitting the ball until one side fails to return the ball. Points are awarded to the serving player or team. When the serving side loses one rally in singles or two rallies in doubles, it loses the serve. Losing the serve is called an *out*. Games are played to twenty-one points. Matches usually consist of winning the best two of three games.

History

Ancient Romans played a version of modern handball called *thermae*. The game appeared in Ireland in the eleventh century, and Spanish and French enthusiasts competed in a game called *pelota*, a version of the sport played without gloves.

Handball was introduced to the United States by Irish immigrants in the 1800s. Phil Casey, called the "Father of American Handball," promoted the sport on the American continent. In 1886, in Brooklyn, New York, he constructed the nation's first handball court upon which he staged a series of handball contests.

One-walled handball appeared around 1920. Although it is still played, most handball contests take place on four-walled courts. It makes for a faster, more thought-provoking game.

The United States Handball Association, formed in 1951, sponsors tournaments and conducts educational programs in hopes of broadening the sport's appeal.

Cutthroat

One version of handball that many players enjoy is called cutthroat. In this version, three competitors square off against each other. The server plays against the other two, and when service is lost the players rotate clockwise.

Cricket

Cricket is a game played with a bat and ball between two teams of eleven players each. The game is extremely popular in England.

Equipment

Twenty-two players compete on an oval grassy field that measures approximately 450 feet (137 meters) wide and 500 feet (150 meters) long. Two *wickets*, or sets of three wooden poles 9 inches (22.9 centimeters) wide and 28 inches (71.1 centimeters) high stand in the middle of the field 22 yards (20 meters) apart. Two sticks called *bails* rest in grooves atop each wicket.

White chalk lines mark off the pitch. A *bowling crease* 8 feet 8 inches (2.64 meters) long runs parallel through both wickets. Four feet (1.22 meters) in front, the *popping crease* marks the line beyond which the *bowler* (pitcher) or *batsman* may not step. Most cricket balls contain a cork center with a leather cover. The ball weighs between 5.5 and 5.75 ounces (155 and 163 grams) and is 8.8 to 9 inches (22 to 23 centimeters) in circumference.

The bat is made of willow with a rubber and wood handle. It weighs about 2 pounds (1 kilogram) and cannot exceed 38 inches (96 centimeters) in length.

Players wear white pants and shirts and white spiked shoes. The batsman and the *wicketkeeper*, a player who squats behind each wicket, wear thick gloves and protective pads on their legs.

A defensive player prepares to receive the ball as the offensive player attempts to run back to the crease in time.

The Event

Games normally last two innings. An inning consists of a complete run through both teams' batting orders.

42

One member of the team at bat stands at each wicket, and this comprises the batting team. The batsman waits for the bowler to bowl the ball, which can be tossed at any speed and may bounce toward the batsman. The batsman attempts to keep the ball from knocking over one of his bails by hitting it with his *paddle*. If the batter thinks that he can run to the other wicket and back before the opposing team retrieves the hit ball, he signals his teammate at the other wicket and the two start running. Should they reach the other wicket, the batsman's team scores a *run*. The players may continue to run back and forth between wickets as long as they choose, but they must reach the opposite wicket before the opponents can knock one over.

An *out* occurs if the bowler tosses a ball which knocks over a bail, if a fielder catches a struck ball before it hits the ground, or if he tries to score a run and the other team breaks his wicket. The winning team is the team with the most runs after two *innings*.

A South African player competes in the first day of his test match at the Lords Cricket Ground in London.

History

Cricket originated in England in the thirteenth or fourteenth century. The first set of written rules was compiled in 1744. In 1787, the Marylebone Cricket Club was formed.

Bowling

The bowler employs many skills to keep the batsman from hitting the ball. He changes the delivery of the ball to confuse his opponent, and he aims at a spot a short distance in front of the batsman. After selecting his spot, he flings the ball at it in hopes of bouncing the ball beyond the batsman.

The English introduced the sport to several continents. By the middle of the nineteenth century the sport had developed an enthusiastic following in Australia, South Africa, the West Indies, New Zealand, India, and Pakistan.

In 1877 the first of what has become the foremost cricket competition, the Test Match, occurred in Melbourne, Australia when an English team challenged an Australian squad. The two nations now meet every four years.

Cross-Country Skiing

Cross-country skiing requires the athlete to race long distances on slightly hilly, snow-covered terrain. Unlike Alpine skiing, the cross-country skier must provide his own propulsion with powerful strides.

Date of Origin
1700s
Place of Origin
Norway
Legendary Performer
Sondre Norheim
Governing Body
Fédération Internationale de Ski
Where They Compete
Worldwide
Championship Events
Olympic Games, World Cup, World Ski Championships

Equipment

Ski boots cover the ankles as a means of support for the athlete. *Ski bindings* hold the boots to the skis, which are the long, narrow blades upon which the athlete glides. The bindings hold down only the front portion of the boot so the skier can easily lift his or her heel as he or she moves. To help provide speed, balance, and give proper direction, the athlete uses *ski poles* made of fiberglass, aluminum, steel, or bamboo. The ski poles end in a sharp point which is surrounded by a circular webbed ring called the *basket*.

Skis are typically made from fiberglass, hardwood, or aluminum. Most skilled athletes use skis that are about 1 foot (30 centimeters) longer than the skier's height.

The Event

Cross-country courses vary in length. Normally, men race in the 15-, 30-, and 50-kilometer (9.3-, 18.6-, and 31-mile) races, while women ski in the 5-, 10-, and 20-kilometer (3.2-, 6.2-, and 12.4-mile) events. Relay races involve four athletes who ski across 10 kilometers (6.2 miles) for men and 5 kilometers (3.1 miles) for women. The courses mix flat surfaces with uphill and downhill portions.

Cross-country skiers rely on a basic movement called the *diagonal stride* to move across the snowy surface. In this action, the skier leans slightly over the front of his skis and moves one ski forward in a maneuver

Cross-country skiing can be practiced nearly anywhere there is snowfall.

44

A cross-country skier executing his diagonal stride.

called the *kick*. The other ski is pulled back and readied for the next kick in a maneuver called the *glide*. As the skier rushes forward, he or she puts pressure on the kick ski to provide a base for shifting weight to the other ski. While shifting from ski to ski, the athlete uses the pole opposite the kick ski to strengthen their forward movement.

Cross-country skiers also employ a movement called the *skate*. In this, the skier pushes one ski straight ahead while thrusting sideways and back with the opposite ski. This gives extra forward thrust and greater speed.

History

Like all Nordic events, cross-country skiing originated in Norway and Sweden, where skiing provided both a method of transportation as well as a source of competition. When Sondre Norheim, a Norwegian, developed improved bindings in the middle of the nineteenth century, athletes were able to perform at a higher level, and Nordic events grew in popularity.

In 1939–40, Finnish soldiers on skis harassed the invading Soviet army and caused the vastly superior enemy more problems than expected. When the United States entered the war, American ski troops successfully battled the Germans in Italy's towering mountains.

Today, an increasing number of people enjoy cross-country skiing as a method of relaxation.

Fact of Life

Skiing is more than a sport in Norway—it is a basic feature of life. Families teach their youngsters to ski before they enter school, and businesses and civic groups conduct ski competitions. One annual race commemorates a historic moment in Norway's past. The Birkebeiner race between Lillehammer and Rena winds through the same route taken 700 years earlier by two Vikings as they carried an infant prince to safety.

Curling

Curling is a game played on ice in which large stones are slid toward targets by two four-man *rinks* (teams). The sport's name comes from the curling action that a player puts on the stone by twisting the wrist at delivery. The game is popular in Australia, New Zealand, and some parts of the United States, but it is widely played in Canada, where 2,000 curling clubs exist.

Equipment

Curling teams use an ice rink that measures 138 feet (42 meters) long and 14 feet (4.2 meters) wide. Each end contains the target, called a *house*, with a *tee* surrounded by four concentric circles used in scoring. The *crampit*, or *hack*, a spiked metal plate from which the athletes deliver the stones, rests 3 to 4 yards (2 to 4 meters) behind the house.

A *curling stone* weighs 42.5 pounds (19.3 kilograms), measures 36 inches (91.4 centimeters) in circumference, and possesses a handle on the top portion which the competitors grasp for delivery. Brooms are used to sweep the ice in front of the stone as it slides toward the house to control the stone's speed. The brooms contain either short, fine bristles or longer, stiffer bristles.

The Event

Each player slides two stones from the crampit toward the house at the opposite end of the rink. Competitors deliver one stone at a time, alternating with their opponents. The players complete an *inning*, or *end*, when all sixteen stones have been delivered. They then move to the opposite end of the rink for the next inning, or end. A typical curling game, called a *bonspiel*, lasts ten ends. Each stone lying closer to the tee than the closest stone of the other team receives a point. Only one team can score points, with eight being the maximum.

Curling players sweep the ice in front of the sliding stone.

Teams deliver stones in a set order. The first member, called the *lead*, is usually the least experienced. Since he or she delivers first, no previous stones rest on the ice to distract the aim. The lead is followed by the number two and number three players.

To deliver the stone, a player puts one foot on the crampit, grabs the stone's handle, slides the stone back along the ice, and gently releases the stone toward the other end with a sliding, twisting motion. The twisting motion allows more control over the stone's direction and speed. The team's captain, called the *skip*, calls out instructions as to whether the ice should be swept in front of the stone to gain speed. Expert sweeping can add as much as 6 to 10 feet (1.8 to 3 meters) to the stone's run.

History

Scotland started the first known curling organization in the sixteenth century. In 1838 standardized rules for the sport were drawn up by members of the Royal Caledonian Curling Club, which today regulates curling throughout the world.

Curling was brought to North America in the early 1800s by regiments of Scottish soldiers stationed in Quebec, Canada. The Royal Montreal Curling Club, thought to be the oldest sporting club in North America, started in 1807.

John Cairnie

John Cairnie's influence on curling is indisputable. In addition to formulating the sport's basic rules, adopted in 1838, he built the first artificial curling pond at his home, Curling Hall. Whenever the weather was perfect for curling, Cairnie hoisted a flag at his residence, indicating to friends that they should come over for a match.

The game appeared in the United States in the 1830s when groups of athletes organized curling competitions in New England and northern Michigan. In 1867 the Grand National Curling Club was formed. Since the end of World War II in 1945, female participation in the sport has dramatically increased.

Curling became an official winter Olympic sport in 1998.

Cycling

Cycling is the sport of racing bicycles, either by individuals or by teams, on tracks of varying distances. It is very popular in Europe, where it is governed by the Union Cycliste Internationale.

Equipment

Racing bicycles are made from lightweight material such as aluminum or titanium. They weigh anywhere from 14 to 21 pounds (6.4 to 9.6 kilograms), depending upon the type of race. The maximum size for bicycles is 6.5 feet long (1.9 meters) and 3 feet wide (.9 meters). They come with light tubular tires, and special pedals hold the rider's feet in place. Riders wear a helmet, a jersey that covers the shoulders, and black shorts that reach to mid-thigh. Goggles and gloves are not required, although racers sometimes use them.

The Event

Track races are the first of four different kinds of bicycle races. Riders compete on either indoor or outdoor oval tracks, which range from 459 to 1,640 feet (140 to 500 meters) in circumference. The course is slightly banked (angled) on the straight portions, and more so at the corners. Track races include quick events such as sprints, which can be as short as 650 feet (200 meters), and longer races up to 31 miles (50 kilometers). The winner is the first athlete to complete the required distance.

Road races wind through city and country streets. This form of cycling, which may involve hundreds of contestants, is the most popular type. Cycling's premier event occurs each year when more than 200 athletes from around the world compete in the Tour de France. The 2,500-mile course is divided into stages, and each cyclist is timed for each stage. The rider with the lowest total time wins.

A road race is generally started in one of two manners. In a massed start, all riders line up at

A photo finish at the 1968 Olympic Games in Mexico City.

the start line and begin at the same time. In a handicap start, the riders' starting positions are determined by how well they raced in earlier events.

Motocross races, often called BMX events (bicycle motocross), began in the 1970s in the United States. Cyclists must negotiate frequent bumps and sharp turns on short, dirt courses. Since many cyclists fall during the demanding event, they must wear sturdier helmets and padded clothing.

Off-road races take advantage of the popularity of the mountain bike in the United States. Mountain bikes are designed with sturdy frames and gears for speeding through mountain paths. Off-road races started in the 1980s and are usually held on dirt tracks.

History

Bobby Julich of the United States pedals his way to the finish line in the 20th stage of the 1998 Tour de France.

The first bicycle was invented in 1839 by the Scotsman Kirkpatrick Macmillan. In 1868, Paris, France, hosted the world's initial bicycle race, won by the English athlete James Moore. The next year, Moore topped more than 2,000 competitors in the first road race, from Paris to Rouen, France.

Henri Desgrange started the Tour de France in 1903. Its prestige has so grown that the winner of each year's event is considered the world's best cyclist.

Men's cycling was included in the first modern Olympic Games in 1896, while female cycling was added in 1980. In the United States the largest race is the annual Tour Du Pont, held each spring in the eastern United States.

A New York Minute

Charles Murphy of New York earned the nickname "Mile-a-Minute" Murphy in 1899 when he became the first rider to pedal one mile in less than a minute. Few believed that a man pedaling a bicycle could attain such speed, but on June 30 Murphy cracked one mile in 57.8 seconds.

Diving

United States diver Cheril Santini in the pike position.

Diving is a sport in which an athlete plunges into the water, either from a *springboard* or a stationary *platform*, with grace and style. In most dives the athlete twists and turns in the air before entering the water.

Equipment

The diving boards used in springboard diving measure 16 feet (5 meters) long and 20 inches (51 centimeters) wide. They extend 6 feet (1.8 meters) beyond the pool's edge, and rest either 3.5 feet (1 meter) or 10 feet (3 meters) above the water.

Diving platforms are 20 feet (6 meters) long and 6.5 feet (2 meters) wide and rest anywhere from 16 to 33 feet (5 to 10 meters) above the water. They are covered by a special nonskid surface, which prevents the athlete from slipping.

The pool must be at least 6 feet (1.8 meters) deep at all spots. The diving area underneath the boards ranges in depth depending upon the event.

The Event

Springboard diving has five different dive groups: the *forward dive, backward dive, reverse dive, inward dive,* and *twist dive* competitions. Platform diving adds a sixth, the *armstand,* in which the athlete balances from a handstand at the platform's edge before pushing off toward the water.

The diver employs one of four different body positions for the dive. The body is kept straight for the *layout position*. In the *pike position*, the body is bent at the waist with the legs straight. In the *tuck position*, the athlete places the legs against the chest and holds the shins with his or her hands. Finally, the *free position* combines elements from the first three body positions.

Women perform five required and five optional dives in springboard competition. They perform four required and five optional dives in platform meets. Men add a sixth optional dive in both cases. The athlete may select which dives to include, but none of the dive groups can be repeated.

Either five or seven judges score the dives based on the approach, the take-off, body movements in the air, and the body position upon entry into the water. The highest score is a ten, while a zero is the lowest. The lowest point totals are dropped, and the remaining scores are added and then multiplied by the dive's degree of difficulty. Any score over a nine is considered outstanding.

History

Competitive diving originated in nineteenth-century Europe, where it emerged as a form of outdoor acrobatics. Gymnastics enthusiasts adapted body movements from their sport and added it to water.

Diving was formally organized in England and the United States in the latter half of the 1800s. Men's diving entered the Olympic Games in 1904. Women's diving followed in 1912.

Patty McCormick was the first American diving star. She was a gold medalist in the platform and springboard events in both the 1952 and 1956 Olympics. She won 77 national championships in her career.

Adele Laurent leaps from an inclined cliff during an international cliff diving competition.

Unique from the Start

Divers use one of three basic starting positions. The diver stands at the springboard's or platform's edge in the standing dive, with the body straight, head raised, and arms either at the side or outstretched. In the running dive, the athlete takes five or more steps before leaping. An armstand dive requires the contestant to assume a balanced handstand before leaving the board.

51

Equestrianism

Equestrianism is a series of events for horse and rider designed to test the horse's development and training, endurance, jumping ability, agility, and grace. Events include local, national, and international competitions.

Equipment

The most common horses used in horse shows are thoroughbred horses. The rider wears breeches and leather boots. Depending on the event, he or she also dons a hard peaked hunt cap, a derby hat, or a top hat. Some riders use a *crop* (whip) with which they gently convey commands.

The Event

Horse shows contain three main types of competition. They are *jumping*, *dressage*, and *eventing*. In the jumping competition, contestants weave through an obstacle course. It entails high jumps over painted poles, brick walls, railway crossing gates, and other impediments. Judges score the horse and rider based upon how gracefully they leap over each obstacle. Points are subtracted for knocking over any part of an obstacle, for falling, and for a horse which balks at jumping.

In dressage competitions, riders direct their horses through different movements. In the *walk*, each of the horse's feet strikes the ground separately. In the *trot* the horse slowly advances with diagonal pairs of legs moving forward in unison. A smooth *canter* shows the horse moving faster than a trot but slower than a *gallop*. Horses are penalized if they move faster than the required speed for each movement.

Points are subtracted when any part of an obstacle is knocked over.

52

Eventing requires that contestants perform in different competitions during a three-day period. After a dressage competition on the first day, the entrants engage in a *cross-country* contest in which they ride over harsh terrain 10 miles (16 kilometers) or longer. The course challenges the horse and rider by containing brush hedges, fences, and streams. The contestants must complete the course within a set time limit. A jumping competition on the third day completes the three-day event. The entrant with the fewest penalties over the three days wins the competition.

History

Riding events have existed for over three-thousand years. Some events originated from the hunt, while dressage has its roots in the training of horses for warfare. The three-day event developed from the difficult marathon races held among cavalry units of European armies. Jumping became popular in the 1800s.

Horses are specially bred for equestrianism and are judged in jumping events on how gracefully they leap over each obstacle.

The Royal Dublin Society in Ireland conducted some of the earliest jumping contests, as did groups in Russia and France. The sport gained popularity in a number of countries toward the end of the nineteenth century.

Charles Mortanges

One noted name from the equestrian world is that of Charles Mortanges from the Netherlands. Over his illustrious career he won five Olympic medals, including individual gold medals in the three-day event in 1928 and 1932 and gold team medals in 1924 and 1928. Mortanges was the first rider to win gold medals in two successive Olympics.

Equestrian events became a fixture in the Olympic Games in 1900. Some of the important equestrian competitions are the international Nations' Cup and the National Horse Show in New Jersey. The American Horse Shows Association regulates the sport in the United States and is affiliated with the Fédération Équestre Internationale.

Fencing

Fencing is a sport in which contestants use their skills with swords to attack opponents and defend themselves. The sport is enjoyed as a collegiate activity and in fencing clubs.

Equipment

Fencers use one of three weapons—the *foil*, *épée*, or *sabre*. The foil is 3-foot (90 centimeter) long, rectangular blade that has a circular guard on the handle. The flexible blade bends when hitting a target. With the foil, a fencer scores points by touching with the sword's tip the opponent's body anywhere in the area from the neck to the hip.

Heavier and more rigid than the foil, the triangular épée is known as the dueling sword. A competitor can hit any portion of the opponent's body with his épée's point.

The sabre is a flexible, triangular blade that is a few inches shorter than the other types. In sabre fencing, touches may be scored with either the sword's tip or with one of the two cutting edges. The hit must land above the opponent's waist.

A fencer wears padded cotton or thick canvas or nylon jackets and knickers. The face is sheltered by a wire-mesh mask with an attached bib covering the neck and throat, while a thick glove protects the hand holding the weapon.

The playing area, also known as the *strip* or *piste*, measures 46 feet (14 meters) long and 6.6 feet (2 meters) wide.

As shown in this 1953 fencing match in Luxembourg, the sabre is flexible and bends when hitting a target.

The Event

The first athlete to accumulate five points wins the contest. Points are determined by electrical scoring devices that register each touch on a fencer's clothing.

Fencers employ a variety of moves. The athlete who first attacks, in a running move called the *flèche*, has the right to continue until either a point is scored or the defender deflects, or *parries*, the attack with his or her own blade. The defender then counterattacks in the *riposte*, and maintains the attack until parried or registering a point.

To maintain proper balance during the match, fencers stand in a slight crouch, with knees bent and feet aligned one in front of the other. The sword is held near waist level. Fencers need strong legs to withstand a match.

Germany's Felix Becker, left, and Peter Cox, Jr., of the United States, duel in their men's individual sabre Olympic fencing match in Atlanta.

History

Guilt and Innocence

In ancient and medieval times a lethal version of fencing was used to determine the innocence or guilt of individuals. As one form of "trial by ordeal," two disputants engaged in a sword fight. According to custom, whoever drew blood first was declared innocent in God's eyes as well as society's. Frequently, drawing first blood meant that the "guilty" party had been killed.

Modern fencing developed in Europe. In the fourteenth century, the sword emerged as the principal weapon in personal combat and most individuals learned how to fight with it.

However, the increasing reliance upon firearms made the sword irrelevant in combat. Swordsmanship was then relegated to the sporting arena. Fencing clubs nurtured the skill, and fencing quickly became an important part of the education of a gentleman. The sport appeared in the first modern Olympic Games, held in 1896.

Field Hockey

In field hockey, two teams of eleven athletes use sticks to hit a ball into their opponents' goal. In the United States, the game is mostly played by women. In other countries, it is popular with both men and women.

Date of Origin	**1100s**
Place of Origin	**England**
Legendary Performer	**Anne Townshend**
Governing Body	**Fédération Internationale de Hockey**
Where They Compete	**United States, Great Britain, India, Pakistan, Germany, Netherlands**
Championship Event	**Olympic Games, World Cup**

Equipment

The playing field measures 100 yards (91 meters) long by 60 yards (55 meters) wide. *Goals*, two 7-foot (2.13-meter) high posts joined by a crossbar that hold a mesh net, stand at each end of the field.

Players carry a *stick* that is curved at the end, flat on the playing (left-hand) side, and round on the other. They may only hit the ball with the stick's flat side. Most sticks are about 37 inches (94 centimeters) long and weigh around 28 ounces (794 grams). A hard outer shell of white leather protects the ball's interior of cork and twine. Balls weigh 5 to 6 ounces (140 to 170 grams) and have a circumference of about 9 inches (23 centimeters).

Players wear a shirt, shorts, stockings, shin guards, and shoes. Only the *goalkeeper*, who must block shots, dons protective gear.

Men's field hockey is very popular in foreign countries such as Pakistan and India.

The Event

The team with the most goals at the end of the game's two thirty-five-minute halves wins the game. A goal is scored when the ball is batted from within the *striking circle* and crosses the *goal line* between the posts. In addition to the goalkeeper, each team fields five *forwards*, three *halfbacks*, and two *backs*.

The game begins with a *passback*. The player from one team hits the ball back from the 50-yard line to a teammate. The squad runs back and forth, advancing the

Players are forbidden to use their sticks above shoulder height.

ball or defending their goal until one team scores.

Only the goalkeeper may use any part of his or her body to stop the ball; the other players are permitted to use only their sticks. Rules require that players advance the ball with the stick. Kicking the ball, picking it up, or carrying it is a violation. The sport eliminates most injuries by forbidding rough play and banning the use of the stick above shoulder height.

History

London schoolboys engaged in a version of field hockey in the twelfth century, and in the next two hundred years young men engaged in frequent matches. The first English hockey club organized around 1840. By 1876 a collection of clubs formed the Hockey Union and wrote a set of rules regulating the sport. International events in field hockey are supervised by the Fédération Internationale de Hockey.

Constance Applebee

Field hockey took hold in the United States when a remarkable English-woman named Constance Applebee introduced the game in 1901. She toured many of the nation's eastern universities, such as Harvard, Vassar, and Smith, to encourage interest in the game, asserting that a "woman cannot be judged until she has performed in field hockey." Because of her work, field hockey gained a place in the American sporting world.

The sport appeared in the United States in 1901 and quickly became a favorite of women. Though men eventually took up the sport in smaller numbers, female stars grabbed the headlines.

The Olympic Games first included men's field hockey in 1908. Women's field hockey, however, had to wait until 1980. Australia and the Netherlands have strong programs, as their women's and men's gold medal victories in the 1996 Olympic Games illustrated.

Figure Skating

Figure skating is the sport in which athletes jump, twirl, or dance on ice, usually accompanied by music. Similar to ballet dancers on ice, they are judged according to the difficulty and gracefulness of their moves.

Equipment

The shoes for figure skating rest upon a broad *blade* .124 inch (3 millimeters) thick and about 1 foot (30 centimeters) long. The blade has an inside and outside edge, allowing skaters to land with their weight shifted to the right or left. Several teeth, called *toe picks*, protrude slightly from the blade's front to enable skaters to dig into the ice as they begin a leap.

Figure skaters wear costumes combining elegance and comfort. Female athletes generally wear a short skirt with tights, while male competitors wear close-fitting pants and matching shirt.

Figure skating competitions are held on *rinks* about 200 feet (60 meters) long and 100 feet (30 meters) wide. A *barrier* about 4 feet (1.2 meters) high surrounds the rink, which has gently rounded corners.

Tara Lipinski became the youngest U.S. national figure skating champion at age 14.

The Event

Figure skaters compete in *singles skating*, *pair skating*, *ice dancing*, and *precision skating*. Judges evaluate figure skaters on a point basis ranging from zero to six, with six being a perfect score. Judges watch for more than grace, for instance, body position during various moves, how the skaters' arms are held, and the difficulty of each maneuver.

Olympic women's figure skating gold medal champion Katarina Witt of East Germany.

Singles skating includes the short skating program and the free-skating program. The short program requires each skater to execute the same three jumps, three spins, and two examples of footwork. The routine must be completed within 2 minutes and 40 seconds. Judges award points in two areas—*technical merit* and *style.*

The free-skating program counts for more in the skater's final score. The four-minute women's and four and one-half-minute men's program is typically filled with more daring leaps and jumps. Figure skaters include their best moves in this part of the competition.

At one time, skaters also had to compete in the *compulsory* figures. More precise than the other forms of competition, compulsories required the athletes to make a figure eight in the ice with their skates, then repeatedly skate over the figure eight without going outside its curves. Because audience and skaters loved the more athletic and graceful programs, compulsory skating was dropped in 1990.

Pair skating teams a male and female skater, who must perform a series of moves as a couple. Some of skating's most spectacular moments occur in this competition. It blends athleticism and daring spins with a romantic element produced by the two coordinating their moves so closely.

During international competition the skaters present only the free-skating program. However, the United States national championships require six pair movements, such as a lift, a solo jump, and a pair spin, in addition to the longer free-skating program.

Ice dancing is more comparable to ballroom dancing than to ballet. Mandatory dance patterns include the Dutch waltz, the tango, and the foxtrot. Judges evaluate the teams on the basis of rhythm, timing, conformity to the music, precision, and teamwork.

In precision skating, teams of skaters synchronize their movements with the music. They are judged on the presentation, originality, and precision of their performance.

History

Though no one can determine the exact origin of ice skating, evidence of the sport dates to 50 B.C. in London, where leather soles and blades fashioned from polished animal bones were discovered in ancient ruins. The world's first skating club appeared in Scotland in 1642. When European settlers arrived in America, ice skating became very popular in the northern United States and in Canada. Modern figure skating dates to 1850, when steel blades became prevalent. These improved blades made it possible for skaters to experiment with spins and jumps.

Russia hosted the first men's world championship figure skating competition in 1896. Ten years later a similar event began for women. Figure skating first appeared in the Olympics in 1908. Today's international competitions are governed by the International Skating Union, founded in 1892.

For a long time European skaters dominated international events. The United States became a force in figure skating in 1914. It conducted its first national competition, consisting of men's and women's singles and pair skating and dancing.

The U.S. Figure Skating Association began supervising American skating in 1921. Up until then, Canadians were allowed to compete, although it was considered the U.S. championships. Since then, they have conducted national tournaments every year. The North American championships started in 1923 and are held every other year.

Sonja Henie

Few skaters affected figure skating like the woman people called the "Norwegian doll." Born in Norway, Sonja Henie practiced eight hours a day starting at age seven, and soon dominated women's figure skating. Henie won ten straight world figure-skating championships and earned three Olympic gold medals. Her grace and beauty made her the darling of the sports world, inspired a line of Sonja Henie dolls, and led to a Hollywood career.

Best of the Best

The first skater to earn international renown was the Norwegian Sonja Henie. She won Norway's championship at age ten.

In the United States, Dick Button first won the United States national title in 1946 at age sixteen, and added Olympic gold medals in 1948 and 1952. He was the reigning world champion for five consecutive years.

Other famed skaters include Scott Hamilton, Dorothy Hamill, and Peggy Fleming of the United States. England's ice dancing team of Jayne Torvill and Christopher Dean popularized that event throughout the world with their sensual, graceful performances. Between 1975 and 1995, the couple won more than twenty national and international competitions.

American figure skater Carol Heiss won four straight national championships from 1957 to 1960, and won the Olympic gold medal in 1960.

In more recent years, Katarina Witt of Germany was the supreme female figure skater during the 1980s. United States competitors Michelle Kwan, Nancy Kerrigan, and Tara Lipinski have all left their mark on skating in the 1990s. Canadians Kurt Browning and Elvis Stojko have dominated the male side of the sport in the 1990s.

An Acrobatic Skater

Few athletes have skated with the flair, daring, and acrobatic style of Canada's Elvis Stojko. Dressed in flamboyant costumes, Stojko thrills audiences with his refusal to back down from difficult jumps. In 1991 he became the first skater to complete a quadruple double combination (four spins, touch down, followed by two spins), and six years later he amazed spectators by landing a quadruple triple combination. His on-ice exploits and athleticism are legendary.

Golf

Golf is an outdoor game in which a player uses *clubs* to hit a small ball into a series of holes. The purpose is to get the ball in the hole in as few swings as possible. After starting in Scotland, the game now has immense appeal throughout the entire world.

Equipment

Golf is played on a plot of land called a *course*. Most courses have eighteen holes. Holes vary in length from about 150 to 600 yards (135 to 550 meters). They contain obstacles which challenge the golfer. Streams, ponds, woods, sand traps (*bunkers*), and thick grass are liberally sprinkled among the eighteen holes.

Golfers begin play in the *tee box*. They place their ball on a *tee* and hit into the *fairway*, which is a stretch of mown grass extending from the tee area to the *putting green*. The putting green is a closely-cut plot of land, generally oval in shape, containing the *cup*. The cup is 4.5 inches (11.3 centimeters) in diameter and at least 4 inches (10 centimeters) deep. It holds the *flagstick*, which serves as a marker at which the golfers aim.

Golfers may use a maximum of fourteen numbered clubs. Clubs are instruments with a thin *shaft*, a *grip*, and a *clubhead* with which the ball is hit. Depending upon the angle of the clubhead's face, the ball flight varies in distance and height.

There are three different types of clubs: *woods*, *irons*, and *putters*. Woods are generally used to hit the ball long distances. Irons are used for controlled shots from shorter distances, and a putter is used on the green. The putter features various forms of clubheads, but they all include a flat surface with which the ball is putted, or hit. Most golfers carry only one putter in their bag.

Ted Tryba posing after his shot.

Sand traps surround greens to make play more difficult for golfers.

A *golf ball* is a sphere consisting of a tightly wound core covered with plastic or rubber. The ball is a minimum of 1.68 inches (4.26 centimeters) in diameter and sports a dimpled surface to enable it to carry longer and straighter through the air.

The Event

The purpose of golf is to play the eighteen holes in as few strokes as possible. The ideal is to shoot *par*, which is the number of shots an expert golfer would take on each hole. Though courses may vary, a typical golf course offers four par-3 holes (par being one stroke with a club and two putts), ten par-4 holes (two strokes and two putts), and four par-5 holes (three strokes and two putts). Golfers generally play in groups of four. There are several different types of competition. In *match play*, the winner is the golfer who wins the most number of holes. To win a hole, a golfer must hole out in fewer strokes than his opponent. If they both hole out in the same amount of stokes, the hole is "halved" and no points are awarded. Match play is featured most prominently in the Ryder Cup, an event which occurs every other year between the best professional golfers from the United States and the best from Europe.

Stroke play is more commonly used by the average golfer and in most professional tournaments. The winner is the person who completes all eighteen holes in the fewest strokes.

After teeing off, the player whose ball is farthest from the hole hits first. He or she must play the ball where it rests without improving its position. The next player to hit is the one whose ball is farthest from the hole, and in that manner all players approach the putting

63

green. On the green, the player farthest from the hole putts first, and he or she has the option of putting again if the ball stops close to the hole.

History

Ancient Romans seemed to have played a game similar to golf called paganica, in which athletes used a stick to hit a feather-stuffed ball. Possibly they introduced their version to local inhabitants when they conquered and occupied the British Isles. Holland developed a game called *het kolven*, which resembled golf; France played *jeu de mail*; and England enjoyed *cambuca*.

English monarchs periodically became worried that the game of golf took too much time from the practice of archery, which they felt was more essential to the defense of the British Isles than a game. At least three different times in the 1400s, kings tried to stifle interest in the game. They failed each time.

Residents of Scotland are credited with inventing the modern game of golf, or *golfe* as they called it. Scottish athletes hit a leather-filled ball over fields that had been used as rabbit runs. In 1744 the first golf club, the Company of Gentlemen Golfers, opened in Edinburgh. Ten years later the Royal and Ancient Golf Club at Saint Andrews, Scotland, developed the first set of rules for the game.

The game grew enormously in the British Isles. So much interest developed that in 1860 the first British Open, the oldest tournament in the world, was held.

Golf spread to the United States in the late 1700s when colonists from Holland imported *het kolven*. The first golf club did not appear until 1888 when Saint Andrews Golf Club— three holes laid out in a cow pasture—opened

What Is Par?

Par varies according to the hole's length. For instance, holes with lengths up to about 250 yards (217 meters) are par-3, those between 250 and 475 yards (217 and 412 meters) are par-4, and those above 475 yards are par-5. A player records a *birdie* when he or she completes a hole in one stroke under par, and a *bogey* if one stroke more than par is required.

Grant Waite uses a long putter to find the bottom of the cup.

in Yonkers, New York. In 1894 the United States Golf Association (USGA) formed, and the next year it hosted the first three United States championships—the Men's Amateur, the Women's Amateur, and the United States Open. Along with the Royal and Ancient Golf Club, the USGA governs golf today.

Best of the Best

Golf in the United States received a huge boost in 1913 when the 20-year-old Francis D. Ouimet outdueled two of England's best players, Harry Vardon and Ted Ray, to capture the United States Open. It enjoyed increasing popularity with the exploits of Gene Sarazen and Bobby Jones in the 1920s and 1930s, and the wizardry of Sam Snead, Ben Hogan, and Byron Nelson in the 1940s and 1950s.

Arnold Palmer captivated audiences in the United States and Europe with his aggressive style of play and dashing looks. In his footsteps appeared the Golden Bear, Jack Nicklaus. Considered by most observers as the best to play the game, Nicklaus won seventy tournaments on the PGA Tour, including an unparalleled eighteen major championships (six Masters, four U.S. Opens, three British Opens, and five PGA's). Young phenom Tiger Woods appears to be following in his path.

Hogan the Hero

Professional golfer Ben Hogan was so seriously injured in a 1949 car accident that doctors feared he would not survive. They certainly believed he would never return to competitive golf. But Hogan was not a man to hear the word "never." In a remarkable recuperation, Hogan again learned to play championship golf. His efforts paid dividends in 1953 when he won three major championships—the Masters, the U.S. Open, and the British Open.

Gymnastics

Gymnastics requires participants to execute acrobatic exercises and other movements with balance, form, and timing. The sport is performed in schools and private gymnasiums, and is practiced around the world.

Date of Origin
Late 1700s
Place of Origin
Germany
Legendary Performers
Friedrich Jahn,
Nadia Comaneci,
Kurt Thomas,
Mary Lou Retton
Governing Bodies
The International
Gymnastics Federation,
USA Gymnastics
Where They Compete
Worldwide
Championship Events
National Collegiate
Championships,
U.S. National AAU
Championships,
Olympic Games,
Pan American Games,
World Games

The Event

International gymnastics includes six events for men and four for women. In both cases the events are performed in a set order, and demand upper body strength, balance, and flexibility. An athlete who enters every event is called an *all-around gymnast*, while those who participate in select categories are called *specialists*.

The events are scored on both an individual and team basis. Judges award points to each athlete depending upon how well he or she executes the required moves. The moves range in difficulty from "A" (easiest) to "E" (most difficult), and the gymnast must include skills from each level of difficulty. A perfect routine receives ten points. Four to six judges evaluate the performances, and the highest and lowest scores are dropped to ensure a fair decision.

In international competition teams consist of six gymnasts. Each gymnast performs in every category, and the team with the highest point total wins. An all-around title is awarded to the gymnast with the highest point total in all six events. Individual titles are given to the athletes with the top score in each event.

Men's Competition

Men begin with the *floor exercise*, which is performed on a 40-foot (12-meter) square mat. The gymnast carries out a series of movements that must be no less than fifty

Dominique Dawes performs her floor routine during the 1996 Summer Olympics in Atlanta. Dawes won the bronze medal in the event.

66

seconds and no more than seventy seconds long. The gymnast may include tumbling, somersaults, hand-springs, and leaps.

The next event is the *pommel horse*. Also called the side horse, the pommel horse is a padded leather piece of equipment measuring 5 feet 4 inches (1.63 meters) long, 14 inches (36 centimeters) wide, and about 4 feet (1.2 meters) high. Two handles, called *pommels*, rest on the center of the horse about 16 inches (40 centimeters) apart. The athlete holds onto the pommels for support as he moves through the routine. Without stopping, the competitor swings his legs in circles around the sides and top of the horse.

The athletes then move on to the *rings*. Two rings 8 inches (24 centimeters) in diameter and 18 inches (54 centimeters) apart are suspended from ropes to a distance of 8 feet (2.4 meters) above the floor. The competitor clutches the rings and attempts to keep them as still as possible while carrying out a series of handstands and circular swings. This event demands incredible strength and balance.

Dominique Moceanu, of Houston, Texas, performs her routine on the uneven bars. Moceanu was a member of the 1996 U.S. gymnastics team that won the gold medal.

The *horse vault* uses a piece of equipment similar to the pommel horse, but without the pommels. The athlete gets a running start and leaps from a *springboard* placed a few feet in front of the horse. He places one or both hands on the horse for support, and vaults over the horse's length. As the athlete soars through the air he executes any one of many moves, such as a somersault or a twist.

The fifth event, the *parallel bars*, requires the gymnast to perform on two bars 11.5 feet (3.5 meters) long, 17 inches (43 centimeters) apart, and 5 feet 5 inches (91.65 meters) from the floor. The gymnast holds onto the parallel bars as he conducts swinging and vaulting movements above and below the bars. The gymnast must include holding positions in which he remains still for a minimum of two seconds.

The *horizontal bar* is performed on a steel bar resting on two metal uprights 6 to 8 feet (1.8 to 2.4 meters) apart. The bar may be raised anywhere from 3 to 8 feet (0.9 to 2.4 meters) above the floor. The athlete swings and vaults from the bar. He sometimes holds on to the bar with one or both hands and other times releases his grip on the bar and then regains it. The gymnast completes this event with an exciting dismount. He builds speed, swings about the bar, lets go, and twists or somersaults in the air before touching the floor.

Women's Competition

Women compete first in the horse vault, followed in order by the *uneven parallel bars*, *balance beam*, and floor exercise. Females use the same equipment as the men in the vault. The major difference is that while men leap over the horse's length, women vault across its width.

In the uneven parallel bars, the high bar stands 7 feet 9 inches (2.36 meters) from the floor and the other stands at 5 feet 2 inches (1.57 meters). In this event, the women athletes switch from bar to bar, all the while completing different moves.

Judging

Though scores at a gymnastics event are based upon 10.0 being perfect, the judges allocate no more than one point. Male competitors start with 9.0, and females with 9.4. From that beginning, judges may award up to 1.0 for men and 0.6 for women, depending upon the performance's difficulty, creativity, artistry, and execution. Judges may also deduct points for faults committed.

A balance beam 14 feet (4.2 meters) long and 4 inches (10 centimeters) wide runs parallel to the floor and is used at heights from 2 to 4 feet (0.6 to 1.2 meters). In a program that must last between seventy and ninety seconds, competitors execute somersaults, jumps, leaps, and turns while maintaining their balance on the narrow beam. Judges subtract points from the score of any athlete who slips or loses balance from the beam during the routine.

The floor exercise for women is similar to the men's, except they perform to music. Judges evaluate the program for athletic skill and for how the style of the routine blends with the music selected. Routines range from 70 to 90 seconds.

History

While gymnastics occurred in other locations, the ancient Greeks elevated the sport to an intense competition. The Greeks emphasized the importance of a healthy body and mind, and constructed special buildings called gymnasiums for citizens. Most young Greek men and women participated in running, tumbling, and rope climbing.

Gymnastics profited from the spectacular display of talent shown by Olga Korbut of the Soviet Union in the 1972 Olympics, and four years later by the Romanian gymnast, Nadia Comaneci. As a result of Mary Lou Retton's gold medal performance in 1984, many young American girls took up the sport. By the 1990s the American female gymnastics team had risen to the top. The U.S. gymnastics team won the gold medal in the team combined exercises in 1996.

Mary Lou Retton raises her arms after performing a perfect 10.0 on the horse vault during the 1984 Olympics in Los Angeles. Retton's achievement won her not only the gold medal in the individual all-around gymnastics event, but also the hearts of the American public.

Absolutely Perfect

Though hundreds of talented athletes had competed in gymnastics, never had a perfect 10.0 score been awarded until the 1976 Olympic Games. A teenager from the Soviet Union, Nadia Comaneci, astounded the world when she received a perfect score in the uneven parallel bars on July 18. Ironically, the scoreboard could not even register her point total because no one thought there was a need for the extra digit. Comaneci went on to win the gold medal.

Hockey

Hockey is a game played on ice between two teams of six players each. The teams attempt to shoot a hard rubber disk (called a *puck*) past the opposing *goalie* into the net. Immensely popular in Canada, the game also has strong followings in the United States and Europe.

Equipment

A regulation ice hockey *rink* is 200 feet (60.9 meters) long and 85 feet (25.9 meters) wide and contains rounded corners. To protect spectators, 4-foot-high (1.2-meter) white wood or fiberglass *boards* surround the rink and support another 4-foot section of safety glass.

Various lines divide the ice surface into sections. Two red *goal lines* run across the ice 10 feet (3 meters) from each end of the rink. In the middle of these goal lines stand the *goal cages*, 4 feet high and 6 feet (1.83 meters) wide. Attached to the two red posts and a crossbar is a white nylon net. A *goal crease* exists immediately in front of the goal. No offensive players are allowed in the crease.

Two wide *blue lines* stretch across the ice 60 feet (18.28 meters) from each goal line. They divide the rink into three sections— the *defending zone*, the *neutral zone* in the middle, and the *attacking zone*.

Nine circles indicate places where play

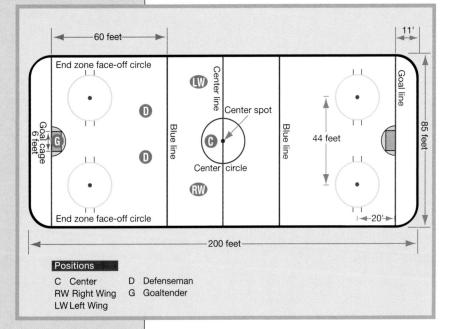

Positions

C Center	D Defenseman
RW Right Wing	G Goaltender
LW Left Wing	

resumes after a halt. The blue *center ice spot*, 1 foot in diameter, rests in the middle of the ice and is surrounded by a *center circle* 15 feet

In a match that is considered one of the most memorable in American sports history, the 1980 United States Olympic team defeated the USSR team 4-3.

(4.6 meters) in radius. Four other similar spots and circles, two in each end, stand near the goal area. Four additional face-off spots 1 foot (.3 meters) in diameter rest inside the neutral zone.

Player's benches are placed behind the sideboards in the neutral zone. Directly across the ice is the *penalty box*, where a player must sit if he or she commits an infraction.

To move the puck, players use a wooden or aluminum *stick* with a blade at the end. The blades may be no longer than 12.5 inches (32 centimeters) nor wider than 3 inches (7.6 centimeters). Goalies use a different stick with a broader surface.

Players wear a shirt, knee-length pants, stockings, heavy leather gloves, skates, and a helmet. Protective equipment is often used, such as elbow and hip pads. Goalies wear face masks, large chest pads, and use a huge glove.

The puck is a hard rubber disk 3 inches (7.5 centimeters) in diameter and 1 inch (2.5 centimeters) thick, weighing about 6 ounces (170 grams).

The Event

Each team places a goalie, two *defenders*, one *center*, and two *forwards* on the ice at any one time. The game, which consists of three twenty-minute periods, begins at center ice. A *face-off*, in which the official drops the puck between two opposing centers, starts the action.

The team with the puck then attacks its opponent. They may move by either one man skating with the puck or by passing it back and forth among teammates. Players may not kick the puck or advance it with their hands.

Teams receive one point each time they shoot the puck into the net. The team with the highest total at game's end is the winner. In the event of a tie, a five-minute overtime is added, and the first team to score wins the game. If the teams remain tied at the end of overtime, a tie is declared. During the post-season playoffs teams continue play until one team wins.

Some of the most exciting hockey takes place when one team plays shorthanded. This occurs when a player is sent to the penalty box by officials for committing an infraction. For a minor infraction, such as tripping or holding an opponent, a player must sit in the penalty box for two minutes. Major penalties bring five minutes. During this time, his teammates must play shorthanded, which gives the opponent a huge advantage. Should the opponent score a goal during that time served, the player may leave the penalty box immediately.

In rare cases a referee may call a penalty shot. This happens when an attacking player is pulled down from behind as he nears the goal area. The player fouled is allowed to skate in on the goalie and take one shot.

Mr. Hockey

While Wayne Gretzky has earned the nickname the "Great One," his own hero enjoys the distinction of being called "Mr. Hockey." In thirty-two professional seasons spread over five different decades, Gordie Howe scored 1,071 goals and assisted on 1,518. In his stellar career he won six scoring titles, six most valuable player awards, and led the Detroit Red Wings to four Stanley Cup championships.

History

Hockey originated from a Native American game played in Canada in the early 1800s. In 1855, when soldiers from the Royal Canadian Rifles organized an informal league of teams near Kingston, Ontario, the game of hockey was born.

Hockey crossed the ocean to Europe in 1907, where amateurs quickly took to the sport. Strong teams arose in Sweden and Russia.

The National Hockey League (NHL) formed in 1917 with five teams—two from Montreal and one each from Toronto, Ottawa, and Quebec. Seven years later the first United States city, Boston, entered the league. Within a few years teams were added from New York, Chicago, and Detroit.

In the 1950s two teams dominated play in the NHL. From the 1949–50 season through the 1959–60 season, Gordie Howe's Detroit Red Wings and Maurice "Rocket" Richard's Montreal Canadiens captured nine of ten Stanley Cups.

The strength, speed, and skill of Eric Lindros makes him the ultimate player package as hockey heads into the millennium.

Best of the Best

Besides Howe and Richard, other players made a big impact on professional hockey. During his tenure with the Boston Bruins, Bobby Orr revolutionized the defensive position with his ability to score and handle the puck. Bobby Clarke of Philadelphia, along with Boston's Phil Esposito, excelled in the rough-and-tough style play in the 1970s. During the 1980s and 1990s, Wayne Gretzky broke almost every scoring record imaginable, and led the Edmonton Oilers to four Stanley Cup championships. Mario Lemieux led the Pittsburgh Penguins to back-to-back titles in 1991 and 1992. Today, players such as Eric Lindros, Peter Forsberg, Jaromir Jagr, Dominic Hasek, and Mike Modano have risen to the top of the NHL.

Gold for the Americans

The 1980 Olympic gold medal in hockey by the U.S. team was called a "miracle on ice." Three teams were rated higher than the United States—the Soviet Union, Canada, and Czechoslovakia. The less-heralded American athletes won a close game with Canada. They upset the Soviet Union 4-3, then grabbed the gold medal by beating Sweden 4-2. The U.S. hockey team hasn't won a medal since 1980.

Horse Racing

Horse racing is a sport that pairs *jockeys* (riders) and horses, in contests matching speed and/or endurance over tracks or courses. The three main types of racing include *thoroughbred racing*, the *steeplechase*, and *harness racing* (which is discussed under "Trotting").

Equipment

In thoroughbred racing, only horses that trace their ancestry to one of three Arabian stallions can be used. The three famed horses, Byerly Turk, Darley Arabian, and Godolphin Barb, were brought to England from the Middle East in the late 1600s and early 1700s. When mated with sturdy English mares, the horses produced offspring combining strength and swiftness.

Thoroughbred horses generally weigh from 1,000 to 1,200 pounds (450 to 544 kilograms) and stand 62 to 65 inches (157 to 165 centimeters) tall from the ground to the *withers*, which is the highest part of a horse's back. Once they reach two years of age, thoroughbreds compete from one to three years before being retired.

Since the total weight of horse, rider, and equipment must not exceed a certain amount, most jockeys weigh around 110 pounds (50 kilograms). Their equipment includes a saddle, whip, boots, safety helmet, white riding pants, and a special jacket and cap called silks.

The Event

Race tracks are oval and are between .5 and 1 mile (.8 and 1.6 kilometers) in length. Tracks in the United States and Canada consist of a loosely raked sandy mixture, while in Europe and elsewhere turf tracks dominate. Bigger horses tend to race better on longer tracks.

The famed horse track Churchill Downs holds the Kentucky Derby each year.

Jockeys withstand rigorous diet and exercise programs to keep their weight down.

Though thoroughbred racing conducts numerous races in the United States and England, each nation has named three events to comprise its Triple Crown, the ultimate challenges for thoroughbred horses. The United States designated the Kentucky Derby, the Preakness, and the Belmont Stakes, while England's Triple Crown consists of the Epsom Derby, the St. Leger Stakes, and the Two Thousand Guineas. The pinnacle of any thoroughbred's career is to win all three races in one year, a feat rarely accomplished.

In steeplechase racing the horse and rider negotiate a series of obstacles as they wind through the course. Contestants in a steeplechase must vault fences, walls, and rails over a 2 to 4-mile (3.2 to 6.4-kilometer) course. The horse will be disqualified if it misses a fence or hurdle, passes the wrong side of a direction marker, or if the rider rides recklessly or jeopardizes another horse's chances. It can also be disqualified if it crosses or interferes with another horse on the home run or at the final hurdle/fence.

History

Modern racing originated in the British Isles by the twelfth century when English knights returned from the Crusades with swift Arabian horses. The fiercely competitive knights and lords loved to organize racing events in which huge amounts of money were wagered.

Racing experts generally consider the best thoroughbred of all time to be either Man O'War, who won twenty of twenty-one races in the 1920s, or 1973 Triple Crown winner Secretariat. Other heralded horses are John Henry, Alysheba, and Citation. The greatest jockey of all time was Willie Shoemaker. By the time he retired in 1990, he had won 8,333 races.

Hurling

Hurling is a sport in which two teams of fifteen each use a stick to drive a small ball through *goal posts*. Beloved in Ireland where it is the oldest sport, hurling is governed by the Gaelic Athletic Association.

Equipment

Players hit the ball with a wooden *hurley stick*, or *caman*, a 3-foot (.91-meter) long stick with a curved, flat end. The horsehide ball is 9 to 10 inches (22.9 to 25.4 centimeters) in circumference and weighs 3.5 to 4 ounces (98 to 112 grams).

The grass playing field is 150 yards (137.2 meters) long and 90 yards (82.3 meters) wide. At each end sits a netted goal 21 feet (6.4 meters) wide with goal posts 21 feet high. A crossbar rests on the goal posts 8 feet (2.4 meters) above the ground.

The Event

Teams consist of a *goalkeeper*, six *defenders*, two *midfielders*, and six *forwards*. Most games last two halves of thirty minutes each. Three points are awarded when an athlete bats the ball by the goalkeeper below the 8-foot crossbar. One point is recorded when the ball smacks into the goal above the crossbar. The team with the most points at the end of regulation time wins the contest.

A player may hit the ball with his hands or kick the ball. If he catches it, he may carry it for no more than three steps. An athlete often advances the ball with the solo run, in which he sprints while balancing or bouncing the ball on his stick's blade. If the ball is on the ground, players must use the stick to lift it into the air. Shoulder-charging is permitted, but tripping, pushing, or pulling is penalized by a free puck against the offender.

Humble Beginning

In August 1884 Michael Cusack gathered a group of athletes in County Galway to organize a number of sports, including hurling. The subsequent Gaelic Athletic Association formulated championship matches for Ireland, and three years later the first Senior Hurling Final took place. Today, more than one hundred thousand play the game in Ireland.

Jai Alai

A lightning-quick indoor game that combines portions of handball, tennis, and lacrosse, jai alai (pronounced *hy ly*) is popular in Florida, Mexico, and Cuba. Tourists visit the professional matches, at which large amounts of money are often wagered.

Equipment

The jai alai court, called a *cancha*, has three walls and measures 176 feet (54 meters) long, 55 feet (17 meters) wide, and 40 feet (12 meters) high. A wire screen stretched across the back open side protects spectators from harm.

Players use a *cesta*, a thin wicker basket about 2 feet (60 centimeters) long, for returning the ball. One end of the cesta has a glove that fits snugly around the player's hand. The opposite end has a basket for catching and throwing the ball. The ball is called the *pelota*. It is made of hard rubber covered by linen thread and two layers of goatskin. The sphere, 2 inches (5 centimeters) in diameter, travels at speeds of 150 miles (240 kilometers) or more per hour.

The Event

As many as eight people play a game of jai alai. Two play on court while the other six wait in turn. The *server* starts the match by flinging the ball against the front wall. The opponent must catch the ball with his cesta either before the ball hits the floor or on its first bounce, and then return it to the front wall. If the player misses, the server receives a point and the player next in line comes out on court; if the server misses, the opponent wins the serve and another player emerges from the waiting line. Games last anywhere from five to seven points. Jai alai originated in the Basque regions of Spain and France, where the game was played as part of celebrations.

After catching the pelota in his cesta, the player prepares for his return shot.

Judo

Judo is a form of unarmed self-defense where contestants try to either pin or throw their opponents off balance. The sport came from the ancient Japanese form of unarmed combat called jujitsu.

Date of Origin
1882
Place of Origin
Japan
Legendary Performers
Jigoro Kano,
Gunji Koizumi,
Yamashita
Governing Body
International Judo
Federation
Where They Compete
Japan,
Europe,
United States
Championship Events
Olympic Games,
World Championships

Equipment

Judo training occurs in a gymnasium called a *dojo*. Contestants wear a *judogi*, a pajama-type outfit consisting of a white cotton jacket and pants and a colored belt. The various colors represent the skill level attained by the judo student, called a *judoka*. Beginner students wear a *white belt* before advancing to a *brown belt*, which indicates the intermediate level. An expert practitioner dons a *black belt*.

Judo techniques are divided into three groups. In *nagewaza*, the student learns hand throws, hip throws, leg sweeps, and side and back throws. *Katamewaza* includes the art of choking and holding. *Atemiwaza* teaches students how to strike vital spots of the body to cause injury or paralysis. This form is used only in self-defense and does not form part of the contest.

The Event

Judo attempts to give students methods by which they can subdue a larger or stronger opponent. The sport teaches an intricate combination of strength, timing, and balance in which the opponent is defeated by his own strength or size. In an effort to simulate combat conditions, judo contests have few rules.

Fighters grip each side of the opponent's jacket, usually on the sleeves or lapels. They grapple for grips but often attempt throws with only one hand on the jacket. A player wins when he or she throws the opponent onto his back with force, or for executing two perfect throws. Victory is also awarded when one player holds

An example of *nagewaza*, the art of throwing your opponent.

78

down his opponent for thirty seconds, or for forcing the opponent to surrender because of an elbow lock or choke hold.

Judo contestants compete in one of two types of judo. In *kata* the contestants perform judo techniques and are judged solely on how expertly they complete each technique. In *randori*, contestants may use any technique they wish to defeat their opponent. The contests last from three to seven minutes.

History

Japanese mythology contends that the ancient gods used jujitsu to punish lawless humans. By the twelfth century jujitsu became a standard form of warfare among Japan's most revered warriors.

France's Djamel Bouras displays the form that won him a gold medal at the 1996 Olympics.

Jigoro Kano, who first used the word *judo*, meaning "gentle way," introduced the sport at his Tokyo school of instruction called the Kodokan. He eliminated the dangerous elements of jujitsu and devised the sport's current rules and etiquette. Kano believed that judo was an excellent form of self-discipline and promoted the notion of "maximum efficiency with minimum effort." Kano opened his first dojo in 1882.

The sport was introduced into the United States in 1902 by one of Kano's top pupils, Yamashita. It spread to England in 1918 when Gunji Koizumi opened a judo school in London.

After World War II ended in 1945, judo enjoyed enormous growth in the United States. In 1964 the sport was included in the Olympic Games.

Center Stage

Judo made its first appearance in the Olympics at the 1964 games held, appropriately, in Tokyo. Japan went to great efforts to ensure that the games unfolded in spectacular fashion, for this was the first time that the Olympic Games had been staged anywhere in Asia. Japanese judo competitors performed brilliantly, capturing three of four gold medals in judo events.

79

Karate

Karate is a form of unarmed combat. It relies on striking one's opponent with either the hands, elbows, knees, or feet. Previously confined to self-defense, karate has expanded into the sport world.

Equipment

The word *karate* means "empty hand," since the participant uses no weapons other than his own body. Most strikes are aimed at vulnerable spots, and in combat an accurate thrust can be fatal.

Though *karate* is known for its martial aspects, it also teaches a lofty moral standard. In facing a dangerous situation, the individual is to refrain from using karate whenever possible, as exemplified by the discipline's motto: "We who can kill must know when our cause is righteous." Only as a last resort should one turn to karate.

Karate involves training the mind as well as the body. Along with being a system of defense and a sport, it is a physical manifestation of Zen Buddhism. Karate is action and Zen is meditation.

Flexibility is integral to performance in karate competition.

Karate divides participants into five classes based upon skill. The color of the belt worn around the athlete's *gi*, or pajama-type costume, signifies the level of achievement attained. A *white belt* denotes a beginner. The student moves through successive ranks—*yellow belt*, *green belt*, *purple belt*, and *brown belt*—until he has attained karate's highest distinction. Only those judged to be such masters of karate may wear the honored *black belt*. Karate training occurs in a *dojo*.

Four main types of karate exist. Korean karate, called *tae kwon do*, emphasizes kicking. The Chinese form, called *kung fu*, places more importance upon a graceful, sweeping motion. Japanese and Okinawan karate feature harsher, more powerful thrusts.

The Event

Most karate tournaments feature matches by age, rank, or weight categories. There are two main types of karate contests. In *form competition*, also called *kata*, each contestant performs different attack forms in front of five judges. *Free fighting*, or *kumite*, pits two athletes against each other. They compete in front of a referee and four judges. A contestant receives a point when the judges determine that he has landed an effective blow. To protect the athletes, the more dangerous karate blows cannot be used and designated portions of the body are off limits. Normally, the head and torso are considered appropriate targets.

Strong will and a bit of a snarl can give the competitor a psychological advantage.

History

Villagers in the ancient Orient developed karate over five thousand years ago as a method of defense against armed bandits. In the 400s B.C. Buddhist monks in India mastered the technique as protection against wild animals.

Karate became prevalent on the Pacific island of Okinawa in the 1600s when a conquering Japanese clan banned the use of weapons. The Japanese quickly integrated karate into their own society and included it as an important feature of military training. Many American military personnel learned the sport while serving tours in the country following World War II.

Silver Screen Sport

Motion pictures and television shows have added to karate's popularity. Stars like Bruce Lee, Chuck Norris, Steven Seagal, and Jackie Chan have glamorized the sport.

Since that time karate in the United States has grown in popularity, both in tournament form and as a method of self-defense. The feature film *The Karate Kid*, made in the 1980s, created an explosion of interest among youngsters in America.

Kickboxing

Kickboxing combines martial arts with boxing. Athletes win matches by scoring more points than their opponents or by knocking them down.

Equipment

Men wear *hakama* (flowing trousers) with *tare* (an apron or groin protector). Female kickboxers wear shorts or baggy pants with a loose top.

Two sizes of *kickboxing gloves* are used. Participants who weigh less than 152 pounds (68.9 kilograms) fight with 8-ounce (227-gram) gloves. Those who weigh more than 152 pounds wear 10-ounce (284-gram) gloves. The gloves cover the top portion of the hand, rather than completely covering the fist as boxing gloves do.

Kickboxers also strap on foot pads. Surgical bandages and tape secure the foot pads. Headgear is required in amateur kickboxing. Mouth guards (to protect teeth) and protective cups (male competitors) are worn as well.

Kickboxing matches occur in a *ring* 16 feet (5 meters) square. Ropes surround the ring, and padded covering softens the floor's surface.

The Event

Athletes compete in seventeen different weight classes, ranging from *flyweight class*, for those 112 pounds (50.8 kilograms) and under, to the *super heavyweight class* for those over 205 pounds (93 kilograms).

Matches last anywhere from five *rounds* of two minutes each to twelve rounds. A one-minute rest period separates each round.

Kickboxing is not simply learning how to fight, but also how to defend yourself.

A demonstrator works out on a "BOB," which stands for body opponent bag.

Contestants score points by successfully landing kicks and punches on their opponent. To avoid the sport's becoming too similar to boxing, professional kickboxers must use at least eight kicks each round, and amateurs must execute six.

Kickboxers win matches either by the judge's decision, or by a knockdown. If an athlete is knocked down and has not risen by the count of ten, the match is awarded to the opponent.

History

Kickboxing has its origins in the ancient Oriental martial art of karate. Karate was a method of unarmed protection against armed bandits in ancient times. It involves striking the opponent with the feet, knees, hands, or elbows.

Despite its origin, the early American version of kickboxing was not full-contact. Kickboxers won points for proper execution of different moves that barely missed the opponent, not for actually striking the other competitor. However, participants and spectators wanted a more aggressive format to promote interest in the sport.

Rules to Fighting

Certain moves are illegal in kickboxing and result in lost points, disqualification, or even suspension from the sport. Banned moves include kneeing, biting, jabbing the eyes, and grabbing the legs. Head-butting also draws a foul.

Karate developed into a full-contact sport in the 1960s, when a karate teacher named Jhoon Rhee developed a set of rules that permitted punching and blocking with the hands and feet. This change led to the development of the current version of American kickboxing. In 1973, Michael Anderson organized the first kickboxing tournament. Since then the sport has spread across the nation.

83

Lacrosse

Lacrosse is a team sport in which a hard ball is tossed about with a long-handled stick. Popular in Canada, it rivals hockey as a national sport.

Equipment

In the United States and Canada the playing field is 110 yards (100 meters) long and from 60 to 70 yards (55 to 64 meters) wide. *Goals* are 6 feet (1.8 meters) high and 6 feet wide. A *net* is attached to each goal. The game's object is to fling the ball beyond the opposing *goalkeeper* and into the net.

The *lacrosse stick* can be anywhere from 3.3 feet to 6 feet (1.5 to 1.8 meters) long and between 7 and 12 inches (17 and 30 centimeters) wide. At one end of the stick, lacing forms a pocket in which to catch, carry, or throw the ball. Players wear helmets, shorts, cleated shoes, gloves, and protective pads on the arms, legs, and body.

The Event

Arm strength and a lengthy reach are beneficial to players on both offense and defense.

Each team fields ten players. A goalkeeper is assisted by three *defenders*, three *midfielders*, and three *attackmen*. Players are not allowed to handle the ball with their hands. Due to the aggressive nature of the sport, body contact plays a big role in men's lacrosse.

Games are divided into four twenty-five-minute *periods*. To avoid a penalty, each team must always have at least three players in the offensive side of the field and four on defense.

Women's lacrosse is played with twelve members on each team. The contestants play two twenty-five-minute *halves*, and body contact is strictly forbidden.

History

The popularity of lacrosse has exploded at the scholastic and collegiate level in the United States.

Lacrosse originated with the Native Americans of eastern Canada in 1636. White settlers saw the Indians playing a game called baggataway. The French called the game lacrosse because the long sticks reminded them of a bishop's staff, called *la croix*.

One aspect that stunned the Europeans was the sport's brutality. Few rules stopped players from adopting any measure, no matter how rough, to advance the ball. One Indian might smash his opponent's head with his stick or attempt to trip him. Rival tribes sometimes sent as many as 500 warriors against an equal number of opponents, and in the ensuing general melee broken arms, legs, and cracked skulls were common. Sometimes, players were even killed in the violent games, which usually lasted several days.

A Game—A Massacre

Rarely has a sporting event been the stage for slaughter, but one such event occurred in Michigan on June 4, 1763. As part of a rebellion against British forces, a group of Native Americans gathered outside Fort Michilimackinac, supposedly to play a game of lacrosse in honor of the king of England. At a prearranged signal, the Indians grabbed hidden weapons and massacred the soldiers, who had relaxed their vigilance to watch the game.

Canadians gravitated to the action-packed sport. When French Canadians picked up the game in large numbers, a group of athletes formed the Montreal Lacrosse Club in 1856. The next year Dr. George W. Beers of Montreal wrote the first formal set of rules for the game.

The game spread into upstate New York and the New England states in 1868. In 1879 the United States Amateur Lacrosse Association formed, and three years later the United States Intercollegiate Lacrosse Association organized the first league.

Luge Tobogganing

Luge tobogganing is a sport in which either one or two competitors lie on their backs on a sled and race down an ice-covered track. The high-speed sport is popular in Europe.

Equipment

Luge tobogganing courses consist of an ice-covered surface and banked sides. The courses must be at least 1,111 yards (1,000 meters) for men's events and 77.8 yards (700 meters) for women's.

Each course includes gradual and sharp turns, which challenge the competitors' skills. The luge may approach speeds of 75 miles (120.6 kilometers) per hour on straight sections.

Athletes use a *luge*, a small sled made of fiberglass or wood fastened atop two runners. Sleds are about 4 feet (1.2 meters) long, 20 inches (51 centimeters) wide, 8 inches (20 centimeters) high, and weigh up to 49 pounds (22 kilograms). Steering is accomplished by applying leg pressure on the *runners* and exerting downward pressure on the luge with the shoulders.

Participants must wear crash helmets, and either goggles or a full-face visor. Skin-tight stretch suits cut down on wind resistance and add speed to the run. Gloves containing small spikes help build momentum for the start.

Aerodynamics affect the speed of luge competitors. They lay as flat as possible with their toes pointed inward.

The Event

Competitors start the race on a horizontal starting area by grabbing handles, or *grips,* set into the ice. They then pull forward to gain acceleration. Once underway, the athletes must remain in the horizontal position for the race's duration.

Most luge tobogganing events require three runs down the course in singles competition and two runs for doubles. The Olympic Games, however, add an extra singles run. The winner is the individual or team that accumulates the lowest total time for all runs.

An athlete may be disqualified for a variety of infractions. The luge cannot exceed a certain weight limit, the athlete must perform a certain number of training runs on the course to familiarize himself or herself with its features, the individual or team must appear at the starting position within the allotted time, he or she may not perform in a hazardous manner during the run, and no outside help can be accepted.

Competitors handle right- and left-hand bends and hairpin bends by applying pressure with their legs and shoulders.

Keep the Heat Off

A luge, or sled, has two steel runners attached to wooden runners which curve upward at the front. Contestants are permitted to wax the runners before a race, but they can be disqualified if they heat them for added speed. Officials inspect the runners before and after the race to ensure that no heating has occurred.

History

Luge tobogganing is mentioned as early as the 1500s, but it first appeared as an organized sport in the late 1800s. Outdoor enthusiasts in the Alps Mountains of Europe raced luges across the snow-covered terrain, and before long special toboggan runs had been fashioned. In 1883, the first international race was conducted, which led to a series of competitions between athletes from various countries.

The first world championships were held in 1955, two years before the formation of the sport's governing body, the Fédération Internationale de Luge de Course. The Olympic Games added luge tobogganing as a sport in 1964.

Motorcycling

Motorcycling is the sport of driving motorcycles along straight, circular, or mixed tracks. The sport is regulated worldwide by the Fédération Internationale Motocycliste.

Equipment

Participants use motorcycles of various engine sizes, depending upon the event. *Road racing bikes* include short *handlebars*, stream-lined *windshields* to protect the rider, and *footrests* toward the back. Road races are conducted over flat, oval *tracks*.

Other racing events, called *motocross*, are held over bumpy, rugged courses, so the machines must be sturdier. The bikes employ special tires for increased traction, wide handlebars, and special absorbers to handle the impact of frequent bumps.

The Events

Because road races are held on relatively smooth surfaces, they place greater emphasis on speed and durability than do motocross events. Drivers in road races reach speeds approaching 200 miles (320 kilometers) per hour on the tracks. The foremost American road race—a 200-mile (320-kilometer) event—is held each year at the famous Daytona International Speedway in Daytona, Florida.

Motocross tosses more obstacles at the biker. Since the course stretches over harsh dirt terrain, the racer must be aware of the course's natural features and the motorcycle's capabilities. *Endurance races*, *hill-climbing events*, and *indoor racing* offer unique thrills to spectators and riders alike.

Racing at speeds approaching 200 miles per hour, bikers seem to defy the laws of gravity.

Spain's Pablo Nieto creates some excitement for spectators.

History

Gottlieb Daimler of Germany invented the first gasoline-powered motorcycle in 1885 by attaching a small internal combustion engine to a wooden bicycle frame.

The United States jumped to the forefront in 1901 by introducing two motorcycles. Both the Thomas motorcycle and the Indian motorcycle were single cylinder machines, but they quickly led to more sophisticated motorcycles. In 1903 George Holden won a race in New York when he covered 10 miles (16.09 kilometers) in just under fifteen minutes for an average speed of 40 miles (64.36 kilometers) per hour.

Motocross racing originated in Europe, where the Alps Mountains and other natural features offered superb settings for motocross courses.

Road racing first appeared in Australia in 1925 when two young motorcyclists raced their motorcycles for the spectators at an agricultural show. The crowds loved the race, and within one year the first permanent dirt racing track opened in Sydney, Australia.

In the mid-1950s, motorcycle racing really took off after the Japanese industry, led by Honda, began a worldwide sales promotion using road racing as a stage for publicity. The exposure Honda received lured other international companies into becoming involved in the sport. Now, advertisements are seen on bikes, windshields, jerseys, boots, and sleeves of the biker.

A Tough Course

One of the most difficult tracks used in motorcycle racing is the famous Snaefell mountain course in Great Britain, which hosts the Isle of Man Tourist Trophy races. Each lap stretches along country roads for a distance of 37.75 miles (60.6 kilometers), contains more than 200 twists and turns, and climbs from sea level to over 1,300 feet (396 meters).

89

Motor Racing

Motor racing is the sport of driving motorized vehicles along circular, straight, or mixed tracks. Many premier events are hosted in Europe and the United States.

Equipment

Motor races mainly consist of a *car*, a *driver*, protective equipment—goggles, fireproof uniform, helmet, gloves—and a *pit crew*. The pit crew is a group of individuals who fine-tune the car before and during the race. Two types of vehicles are primarily used in motor racing: single-seat, mid-engine vehicles called *Formula One cars*, and *stock cars*. Stock cars are vehicles assembled from parts purchased over the counter.

Cars must have no more than four road wheels, a complete floor, a protective bulkhead between engine and driver's compartment, and be fitted with spring suspension between the wheels and the chassis.

The Events

The Grand Prix circuit of eighteen to twenty annual events dominates European motor racing, and the driver each year who totals the most points in these events is labeled the World Champion. Only Formula One cars are permitted in these events. Some races wind through the city, while others occur on special *tracks*. Cars travel up to 180 miles (290 kilometers) per hour in these races.

The famed Indianapolis 500 is run on an oval track 2.5 miles (4.02 kilometers) in circuit. Drivers must complete 200 laps. The event is hosted by the Championship Auto Racing Teams (CART).

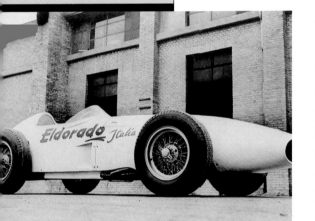

A specially built Italian Maserati Eldorado, which British motor racing king Stirling Moss drove in the 500-mile Grand Prix at Monza in 1958.

The fastest-rising racing event is the stock car racing circuit. A uniquely American creation, a stock car is any vehicle assembled from parts that can be purchased over the counter. Formula One cars are specially adapted vehicles. Extremely popular in the southern United States, stock car racing is supervised by the National Association for Stock Car Auto Racing (NASCAR).

Other types of racing include *drag racing*, *off-road racing*, and *speed trials*, where a driver attempts to break a speed record.

Michael Schumacher cruising his Ferrari to victory in the pouring rain at the British Grand Prix in 1998.

History

Automobile racing started in Europe in 1894 when Frenchman Pierre Giffard organized a road test for horseless carriages. The next year the first organized road race occurred when twenty-two cars entered the Paris-to-Bordeaux race. This created a boom in town races and led to a series of events called the Gordon Bennett Races.

In the United States, Frank Duryea won the first organized race in 1895. In 1911, Indianapolis hosted its first 500 race.

A Lengthy Travel

A ten thousand-mile road race from Beijing to Paris captured attention in 1907. Held over large sections of terrain that had not even been mapped, the winner arrived in Paris two months after leaving China, defeating the second-place finisher by three weeks.

Daytona Beach, Florida, hosted the first stock car race in 1936. Eleven years later, NASCAR began overseeing events.

While the Indianapolis 500 captured headlines, stock car racing emerged as an exciting format of its own. Under NASCAR's guidance, the sport grew rapidly. Today, drivers like Jeff Gordon, Mark Martin, and Dale Jarrett draw countless fans to the tracks.

Nordic Skiing

Date of Origin
1860
Place of Origin
Norway
Legendary Performer
Sondre Norheim
Governing Body
Fédération Internationale de Ski
Where They Compete
Europe, North America
Championship Events
Olympic Games, World Cup, World Ski Championships

Nordic skiing consists of two main forms of snow skiing—*cross-country skiing* (discussed under its own entry) and *ski jumping*. The sport received this name because the term Nordic refers to northern Europe, particularly the nations of Norway, Sweden, and Finland, where these forms of skiing are popular. In recent years *freestyle skiing*, a variation of ski jumping, has gained prominence.

Equipment

Jumping skis are the longest in the sport, normally reaching 94 inches (240 centimeters) in length. To add correct speed, balance, and give proper direction, the athlete uses *ski poles* made of fiberglass, aluminum, steel, or bamboo. Freestyle skiers use a longer, stronger pole because it must support the athlete as he or she executes somersaults and other stunts. To avoid serious injuries during spills, the *ski bindings* release the skis whenever the athlete falls.

The Event

In jumping competitions, the skier propels himself down a long ramp called the *in-run*. He lifts into the air with as much spring as possible, and strains to reach maximum length for his jump. He lands on a slope that angles downward called the *out-run*. Most ski jumping occurs on 90- and 120-meter (296- and 394-foot) hills.

Athletes receive points for the jump's length and for the jumping style, which includes the form maintained while in the air and balance upon hitting the ground. Jumpers lean forward into a nearly horizontal position and land with one foot in front of the other. Some jumpers have leaped well over 300 feet (91 meters), or longer than an American football field.

Nordic ski jumping is judged not only on distance, but also on maintaining form while airborne.

Freestyle skiing differs from ski jumping in that, before landing, skiers are expected to execute spins, somersaults, and other maneuvers. Competitors are judged on the difficulty of their program and how well they execute it.

Mogul freestyle skiing occurs on a steep slope containing numerous mounds, called moguls. The word "mogul" is formed from the "mo" in "mountains" and the "gul" in "gullies." While skiers speed down the bumpy hill, they must perform two upright jumps. Athletes are judged on their maneuverability, the height and execution of their two jumps, and how fast they are able to complete the course.

Ballet freestyle skiing is similar to figure skating in that the competition performs a program of spins and somersaults while accompanied by a musical score.

Though less dramatic, cross-country skiing is coupled with ski jumping in the *Nordic Combined* event.

Ski jumping is also included in the Nordic Combined event. This contest combines jumping with a cross-country race.

History

Pop on Skis

Norway's Sondre Norheim earned the nickname "Father of Ski Jumping" in 1860 when he completed the first officially measured ski jump. He also improved the sport by creating a new binding that wrapped around the heel and gave the performer more control over the skis.

For many years Scandinavian nations dominated Nordic events at both international and Olympic contests. However, in the 1960s, other European countries and the Soviet Union (now Russia) offered stiff competition. Skiing's foremost competitions are the World Championships and Olympic Games. The World Championships are sponsored by the Fédération Internationale de Ski (FIS), which coordinates every international event besides the Olympics.

93

Paddleball

Paddleball is played on a one-, three-, or four-wall *court*. Players hit a hard rubber ball against the front wall and hope the opponent cannot successfully return the hit to that wall before the ball bounces twice on the floor.

Equipment

Paddleball players use a wooden paddle approximately 16 inches (40 centimeters) long and 8 inches (20 centimeters) wide. With the paddle, they smack a hard rubber ball 1.8 inches (4.8 centimeters) in diameter.

The most common paddleball court is the enclosed four-wall court. It measures 20 feet (6 meters) wide and 40 feet (12 meters) long. A 20-foot (6-meter) high front wall is connected to the 14-foot (4.3-meter) high rear wall by side walls.

Various white lines mark different zones on the court. The *short line* runs across the court's middle, and 5 feet (1.5 meters) in front runs the *service line.* The *server* must stand between these two lines.

One-walled courts are used outdoors. The court measures 20 feet (6 meters) wide by 34 feet (10 meters) long. In addition to the short line and service lines, a *long line* marks the back end of the court.

Three-walled courts have the same measurements as a one-walled court, with one main addition. The two side walls slope downward from the front wall's top edge to the short

Spain's Prime Minister José María Aznar returns a shot during a recent paddleball match. Aznar is a big fan of the game.

line. Those walls should be 6 feet (1.8 meters) high at the short line.

Rules forbid a competitor from *hindering*, or blocking, the other side from reaching the ball. If this happens, no point is awarded and the service is repeated.

Any type of outfit can be worn. In official tournament play, white or light clothing is preferable. Doubles partners must wear similar outfits. Knee and elbow pads may be worn.

The Event

The server bounces the ball and hits it to the front wall. If it carries beyond the short line, it's in play. The opponent must return the ball before it hits the floor twice. A shot may hit any of the walls, as long as it strikes the front wall before hitting the floor. Points are only awarded to the server. Games are played to twenty-one points.

One strategic maneuver in paddleball is to hit the ball so low to the bottom of the front wall that the opponent has no hope of returning it. This shot is called a *kill shot*.

History

Paddleball evolved in the 1930s from the sport of handball, whose participants sometimes developed sore hands from hitting the hard ball with their gloved hands. Earl Riskey, the director of intramural sports at the University of Michigan, created paddleball as an answer. The game includes the same competitive features and rules of handball, but players could use a paddle. Army personnel training in the 1940s, during World War II, picked up the game and spread it to other parts of the nation. The sport's governing body, the National Paddleball Association, formed in 1966.

Polo

Polo is an indoor or outdoor game played on horseback in which two teams of four players try to hit a ball through their opponents' *goal posts*. Great Britain, the United States, and Argentina excel in the activity.

Date of Origin
1862
Place of Origin
India
Legendary Performers
Larry Waterbury,
Monty Waterbury,
Devereux Milburn,
Harry Payne Whitney
Governing Body
United States
Polo Association
Where They Compete
Europe,
South America,
United States
Championship Event
Cup of the Americas

Equipment

The regulation *polo field* has a maximum measurement of 300 yards (274 meters) long and 200 yards (183 meters) wide and is surrounded by a *safety zone* or encased by wooden *sideboards*. The goals consist of two goal posts standing 8 yards (7.3 meters) apart.

Players carry *mallets* from 48 to 54 inches (122 to 137 centimeters) long. They hit plastic or wooden balls that are 3 inches (7.6 centimeters) in diameter. The mallet has a solid wooden head, flexible shaft, and a strap that fastens to the player's thumb.

Participants must wear a hard polo helmet for protection. They also wear boots, white breeches, knee guards, and colorful jerseys. Each player uses several horses in a match.

The Event

Matches are usually divided into four or eight seven-minute periods called *chukkers*. Mounted officials may assess penalties for many offenses, including misusing a mallet or trying to trip an opponent's horse. Depending upon the seriousness of the infraction, officials may award free shots at the goal.

The two *forwards* carry the action to the opponent's goal. A third rider works on both offense and defense, while the fourth man serves as the *goalkeeper*.

Prince Charles plays polo during a charity match in Buenos Aires.

Most matches use a handicap system ranging from 0 to +10 to assure fair competition. A superb team may carry a handicap as high as +10, while an inexperienced team may have a handicap of only 0. The difference in handicaps is awarded to the team with the lower handicap. For instance, if one team carries a handicap of +5 and the other has +2, the second team begins the game with a three-goal lead.

History

Polo is said to have been started 4,000 years ago in Persia, or present-day Iran. The game spread to India where it was played by enthusiastic village people. Polo had very few rules until 1862, when British soldiers began to modify it. With a new set of rules, polo soon became popular among the elite of England.

The first international competition occurred in 1886 when a team from the United States challenged an English squad. In the 1930s, Argentinian teams entered the scene and have been a major factor in the sport ever since.

A player's mallet is approximately 4 feet in length.

A Royal Matchup

Through the ages, polo has been avidly played by world conquerors, kings, and lesser rulers. Alexander the Great of Greece received a polo stick as tribute for conquering vast lands, and the sixteenth-century Mogul emperor Akbar the Great relaxed with frequent polo contests.

International play does not occur on a regular basis because of the high cost of shipping horses abroad. The premier international event, the Cup of the Americas, pits Argentina against the United States and takes place whenever one country challenges the other. The United States Polo Association, formed in 1890, conducts annual indoor and outdoor tournaments in that nation. The tournaments include the National Open Championships and the Twenty-Goal, Twelve Goal, and Intercircuit championships.

97

Powerboat Racing

Powerboat racing is the sport of speeding across water in motor-boats. Racing events fall into one of two classifications—*outboard racing* and *inboard racing*. The sport is popular all over the world.

Equipment

Racing boats range in length from 9 to 50 feet (2.7 to 15 meters). Outboard motorboats use special marine engines developed for high performance on water. The engine, propeller drives, and fuel tanks are attached outside the hull to the boat's stern, or rear. Inboard racing boats feature these elements inside the boat's hull.

Racing boats sport either *displacement hulls* or *planing hulls*. Displacement hulls have flat bottoms with sloped sides. The driver either sits (for inboards) or kneels (for outboards) in front of the engine.

Planing hulls are much flatter. The most common form, the *hydroplane*, skims along the water's surface instead of settling slightly into the water. Speeds approaching 200 miles (320 kilometers) per hour are reached by some of the more powerful hydroplanes.

The Event

Organized in 1903, the American Power Boat Association (APBA) sanctions four different types of races. In the *closed-course*, or circular race, boats speed around circular or oval courses of varying lengths, normally 5 or 6 miles (8 or 10 km) long.

Endurance, or *marathon, racing* most often occurs on a circular course. Drivers either finish as many laps as possible in a set amount of time, or they race to be the first to complete a set distance ranging from 50 to 100 miles (80 to 160 kilometers) in length.

A drag powerboat race held in Dunaujvaros, Hungary.

This offshore powerboat completed a 359-mile trip in 3 hours, 43 minutes, 52 seconds, averaging 96.7 miles per hour.

Drag racing by motorboats is similar to automobile racing. From a complete standstill in the water, drivers accelerate their boats and dash down a straight line course generally a quarter mile long.

A fourth type of powerboat racing, *offshore racing*, occurs in ocean waters and can cover 200 miles (320 kilometers). Offshore powerboat racing in American waters is performed mostly by professionals. A major powerboat competition in the United States is the Gold Cup series. High-powered hydroplanes compete each year in hopes of capturing the Gold Cup.

Another form of powerboat racing is *predicted log racing*. Though this type of race is not nearly as fast, it requires a high level of seamanship. Amateur skippers predict the time it will take their cruisers to cover a given route while taking into consideration winds, current, and navigational hazards.

History

Safety First

In addition to helmets, powerboat drivers wear life jackets with special collars to help prevent neck injuries. Also, to protect any driver who is tossed from the craft, a "kill switch" is connected to the life jacket. When the switch becomes detached from the jacket, the engine automatically shuts down to prevent the driver from being run over by the boat.

By the late nineteenth century, almost every possible rowboat and sailboat design had been tried. In 1887, German Gustav Daimler invented the first gas engine–powered boat. He attached an engine to a rowboat and navigated about France's Seine River. It wasn't until the 1890s that Daimler and fellow German Karl Benz developed a powerboat that was commercially affordable.

Boating competition has led to more powerful outboard engines.

Rodeo

A rodeo celebrates the skills used by cowboys such as roping and riding. Coming from a Spanish word denoting a roundup of cattle, rodeos attract enthusiastic crowds throughout the United States and Canada.

Equipment

Depending on the type of rodeo competition, events include horses, bulls, steers, broncos, and calves. Competitors wear blue jeans, cowboy boots, and a cowboy hat. Rope is used to tie down animals and events take place in a dirt ring.

The Event

Rodeo competitions fall into two categories. *Rough stock events* feature competitors who ride bucking horses or bulls. In *timed events*, contestants receive points for the speed with which a requirement is performed. Most rodeos include three rough stock events and five timed events.

In *bareback bronco riding*, the contestant rides a bucking horse without a saddle for eight seconds. The rider grasps with one hand a leather strap that is attached to the horse. In *saddle back riding*, the rider must keep one hand in the air at all times and both feet in the stirrups. The goal is to stay on the horse for eight to ten seconds. In *bull riding*, competitors attempt to remain on a bull for eight seconds by clutching an unknotted rope looped around the bull's neck. This is considered the most dangerous event because of the bull's ferocious temperament and strength.

Saddle bronco riding can be traced back to the Wild West.

The first timed event is *calf roping*. The cowboy must rope a calf, leave his horse, and tie any three of the calf's feet. In *steer wrestling*, the cowboy rides alongside a steer, leaps from his horse and wrestles it to the ground. *Steer roping* requires a mounted competitor to rope a running steer around its horns, nudge the horse behind the steer to the other side, and trip the steer with the rope. The contestant then dismounts and ties the animal's hind legs together.

History

Rodeos appeared during the American Wild West days of the 1800s. Cowboys placed bets on competitors, then filled the afternoon watching the entrants perform. In 1888, the first rodeo competition was held in Prescott, Arizona.

In 1936, cowboys formed the Cowboy Turtles Association to regulate the sport. Now called the Professional Rodeo Cowboys Association (PRCA), the organization supervises rodeos across the North American continent. The most famous rodeos are the Frontier Days Celebration in Cheyenne, Wyoming, the Calgary Stampede in Canada, the California Rodeo in Salinas, and the National Finals Rodeo in Oklahoma City, Oklahoma. The top fifteen money winners of that year compete at these rodeos. Once only a man's sport, all-female rodeos have appeared in recent years.

Life on the rodeo circuit can be demanding. Due to the alarming number of broken bones, serious slashes, and bruises, each contestant must sign a legal document releasing the organizers from any responsibility for injuries. Cowboys compete in rodeos for only a few years.

Once the gate opens, cowboys tightly grip the leather strap and hold on for dear life.

Crazy Cowboy

The most unique rodeo cowboy was Bill Pickett, who developed a routine for wrestling steer to the ground that few, if any, competitors tried. Pickett rode alongside a steer, jumped onto its head, and grabbed a horn with each hand. He then twisted the horns until the steer's nose pointed up, at which time Pickett bit into the steer's upper lip, dropped to one side, and held on until the steer dropped from exhaustion.

Rollerblading

Rollerblading, also known as in-line skating, is one of the fastest growing sports among outdoor enthusiasts. It can be done almost anywhere by people of all ages.

Equipment

The rollerblade skates rest upon either three or four wheels. Wheels are soft in texture for beginners and harder in texture for racers and roller hockey players. One or both skates also have a brake, which is a rubber block on the skate's rear portion. To stop, skaters lean back and scrape the rubber block along the pavement.

Many skaters wear protective gear. This includes a helmet, elbow pads, and knee pads. Because it takes some time to become an efficient skater, and it's easy to take a spill, protective gear is recommended for all participants.

The Event

The world's best in-line skaters can be seen at the X-Games, which is broadcast on ESPN.

Rollerblades are used in a variety of competitive events. Many athletes speed skate with special blades containing five wheels. Races are either *quick sprints* down straight paths or *long-distance races* stretching up to 18.6 miles (30 kilometers).

Other athletes engage in *extreme skating*. This includes a variety of jumps and maneuvers.

Many extreme skaters ride ramps because it allows them to attain heights to execute twists and turns. The ramp, called a *half pipe*, allows the skater to move back and forth to gain the necessary momentum to perform a trick. Extreme skaters possess great balance, agility, and aggressiveness.

Another popular form of rollerblading is *roller hockey*. Some of the rules that distinguish it from ice hockey are that there are no *off-sides*, and a team gets a *free hit* when the opposing team strikes the ball out of the playing area, called the rink. The game is played with a ball that weighs 5.5 ounces (156 grams) and measures 9 inches (23 centimeters) in circumference. It's made of compressed cork. Many cities in the United States have installed roller hockey arenas to offer a place for kids to play year-round.

History

Most observers claim that Englishman Joseph Merlin invented the first rollerblade in 1760 when he attached wooden wheels to leather shoes. Modern in-line skates were created in 1980 by Scott and Brennan Olson of Minneapolis, Minnesota.

In 1991, the International In-Line Skating Association (IISA) was formed to supervise the sport. The IISA trains people to become in-line skating instructors and works to improve relations between skaters and city leaders.

Competitive forms of in-line skating started in 1994 with the National In-Line Skate Series. Professional events are now sanctioned by the Aggressive Skating Association. At the 1996 Atlanta Summer Olympics, in-line racing was included as an exhibition sport. Roller hockey is governed by USA Hockey, the same organization which oversees ice hockey.

Rollerblading is also a recreational sport for kids of all ages.

Rules to Live By

While fun, rollerblading can be dangerous if precautions are not taken. The International In-Line Skating Association devised ten rules for participants. Their first rule warns the individual to wear protective gear. Others tell the skater to skate on the right side of the path or sidewalk, skate under control, yield to pedestrians, and stay away from water, oil, and debris.

Rowing

Rowing refers to the act of propelling a boat with oars. Popular around the world, rowing particularly flourishes in England, Canada, the United States, and Australia.

Equipment

The boats, called *shells*, vary in size, shape, and width. Boats range from 28 to more than 61 feet (8 to 18 meters) long and 25 to 280 pounds (11 to 130 kilograms), depending upon the number of *rowers*. Seats for rowers rest upon rollers on metal tracks so the rower can move forward and backward as he rows for extra force. *Footrests*, bearing built-in shoes, sit about 15 inches (38 centimeters) in front of each seat.

Two main types of rowing exist in competition—*sweep oar rowing* and *sculling*. In sweep oar rowing, each person uses one oar. The boat holds either two, four, or eight rowers. Most boats also contain a *coxswain*, who steers the boat and directs the rowers' strokes.

In sculling, each rower uses two oars. The boat, called a *scull*, normally holds either one, two, or four rowers.

Each person uses one oar in sweep oar rowing as the coxswain (right) steers the boat and screams commands.

The Event

Racing meets, called *regattas*, are held worldwide and are supervised by the Fédération Internationale des Sociétés d'Aviron. Many contests offer races for different weight classes for both men and women. The most famous racing event is England's Henry Royal Regatta, which has been held each July since 1840 at Henley-on-Thames. The distance for all Henley events is 1 mile 55 yards (2,112 meters).

The goal during the *stroke* is to move the boat as far and as fast as possible. When the blade is out of the water, the object is to do as little as possible to hinder the acceleration and run of the boat. A racing rate for a *crew*, or team of rowers, will be between 32 and 40 strokes per minute. For scullers, it is a bit less.

The United States hosts over 200 regattas each year, and the sport has become popular in many colleges. The oldest intercollegiate event is the Harvard-Yale regatta, conducted over a 4-mile (6-kilometer) long course.

Teamwork is the single most important element to a successful rowing team, or crew.

History

England's oldest rowing event, the Doggett's Coat and Badge Race, began in 1715. Sponsored by one of the nation's most popular comedians of the day, Thomas Doggett, the event is still held today. The race is conducted over a 4-mile (6-kilometer) course on the Thames River, from London Bridge to Chelsea.

Boat racing traveled to America with English colonial settlers. The first race was held in New York City in 1811. Intercollegiate racing started in 1852 when Harvard defeated Yale on New Hampshire's Lake Winnepesaukee.

Rowing and sculling have been held at the Olympic Games since 1900. Events include single sculls, double sculls, lightweight double sculls, quadruple sculls, coxless pair, coxless four, lightweight coxless four, and eight-oars.

Slave Labor

In ancient times rowers faced a bleak existence, for they frequently were galley slaves. Chained to their posts below decks, the rowers powered huge Greek and Roman warships. When Roman invaders conquered England, they passed on their rowing skills to the native Britons. Later, English rowers were free men earning money. Many of them plied English rivers as an early form of the taxicab.

Rugby

Rugby, the predecessor to American football, is a running, kicking, and passing game between two teams of fifteen players. The sport originated in England, where it is still popular.

Equipment

A *rugby field* carries a maximum width of 75 yards (69 meters) and length of 157 yards (144 meters). Opposing *goal lines* rest 109 yards (100 meters) apart, and behind each lies the *in-goal*, an area up to 24 yards (22 meters) deep.

A *goal post* stands on each goal line. The posts, 6.1 yards (5.6 meters) apart, are joined by a crossbar 33.3 yards (3 meters) from the ground. The *rugby ball* resembles an American football, but is thicker in the middle. While easier to kick, the ball is difficult to pass.

Players wear simple uniforms of shorts, shirts, and cleated shoes.

The Event

Two types of rugby exist—the amateur version called *rugby union*, and a professional version called *rugby league*. The object is to score points in one of four ways. Three points are awarded for a *try*, which occurs when a player crosses the opponent's goal line. Two points are won with a *goal*, which happens following a try when a player kicks the ball over the crossbar between the uprights. Should the player *drop kick* the ball over the post during action, three points are awarded. A team also receives three points if it successfully executes a *penalty goal*.

It's no secret the sport of rugby can be devastatingly painful.

A Rugged Sport

Amateur squads field fifteen men— eight defensive men called *forwards*, and seven attackers called *backs*. Professional teams use only six forwards. The athletes must be physically strong to absorb the rough style of play without padding, agile to handle the ball in any one of three ways (run, kick, pass), and they must be swift to avoid the other team's players and advance near the goal line.

The game is split into two forty-minute *periods*. No substitutions are permitted, except in international matches.

Rugby play continues nonstop until either team scores, a penalty is called, or the ball goes out of bounds. Athletes advance the ball by running, kicking, or passing it (forward passes are illegal). If one player is tackled, he must immediately release the ball, and the ball can be picked up by the nearest player on either side. The two teams try to advance the ball close enough to the opponent's goal line to either run it in or kick the ball over the crossbar.

Should the ball bounce out of bounds, the teams form a *line-out*. Eight players from each side form two parallel lines about 2 feet (0.6 meters) apart. A player from the team opposing the one that last touched the ball throws it between the two lines, which rush forward and fight for possession. When play is stopped by a rules infraction, the referee calls a *scrum*. Each player lines up, but in a 3-2-3 formation. The ball is dropped and the teams scramble for possession.

History

Rugby started during an 1823 soccer match played at Rugby School in Rugby, England. In the middle of the contest, a student illegally picked up the ball and ran with it. Gradually, other athletes incorporated this tactic into a new game named rugby.

In 1895, teams from northern England established The Northern Rugby Union, which evolved into the professional version. The International Rugby Board was organized in 1948 to supervise both the Rugby Union and the Rugby League.

In the United States, rugby is popular among universities as a club sport. The University of California at Berkeley has dominated the Men's Rugby National Championships since 1991.

Shooting

Shooting is a competitive sport in which contestants shoot at targets. It is performed both indoors and outdoors worldwide.

Equipment

Three types of firearms are used in shooting—*rifles*, *pistols*, and *shotguns*. Rifles and pistols are generally used to shoot at stationary *paper targets*. Shotguns are fired at *clay targets*, which are propelled into the air from a machine. The paper targets vary in size depending upon whether the contest is indoor or outdoor.

The Event

Rifle shooting contests are divided into *small-bore* (.22 caliber) and *big-bore events*. Both entail firing from four positions—lying on the ground, sitting, kneeling, and standing.

Small-bore rifles are more widely used in competition, with outdoor targets placed 50 or 100 yards (45.7 or 91.4 meters) away from the shooter. Targets stand 50 feet (15.2 meters) from the shooter. Targets contain six *rings* with a *bull's-eye* in the middle.

All small-bore events are *slow-fire events*. Contestants have one minute between shots, and the winner is the one who compiles the highest point total. Events are also divided into those permitting *telescopic sights* and those allowing *metallic sights*.

Competitors in big-bore, or high-powered, events must fire a certain number of shots in a set time period, or a series of ten-shot strings within fifty, sixty, or seventy seconds.

Peering through a scope, the shooter takes aim at his target.

Targets are placed at distances ranging from 100 to 1,000 yards (91.44 to 914.4 meters).

Pistol shooting occurs both indoors and outdoors. For outdoor competition, the targets rest 25 or 50 feet (7.6 or 15 meters) from the shooter, and 50 feet for indoor events. Entrants use either a .45-caliber pistol, 38-caliber revolver, or .22-caliber pistol for outdoor competition. They may only fire the .22-caliber pistol indoors. All shooting is done from the standing position.

Shotgun events include *trapshooting* and *skeet shooting*. The shooter receives twenty-five shots at saucer-shaped targets called *clay pigeons*.

In trapshooting, the pigeon is launched from 16 yards (14.6 meters) in front of the shooter in a direction heading away from the shooter. The entrant fires five shots from each of five stations. In skeet, shooters fire at targets launched from either end of a semicircle 120.75 feet (36.8 meters) across.

History

Shooting contests began shortly after firearms became widespread in the 1700s. One military shooting club existed in Geneva, Switzerland in 1774.

Colonial and frontier riflemen in the United States organized contests, but use of rifles in sporting events did not become organized until the early 1800s.

In 1903, the first national rifle matches occurred. True shooting competition did not start until after World War I (1914–18). Under the guidance of the National Rifle Association, the event takes place each year. The Olympic Games carries ten different shooting events in the men's competition and five events for women.

Skateboarding

Skateboarding is a sport in which an athlete performs different maneuvers while riding a small, four-wheeled board. Skateboarding is most popular in the United States.

Equipment

A skateboard has two wheels made of strong plastic mounted on a front axle and two similar wheels mounted on a rear axle. Both sets can pivot on their axles. A board, called the *deck*, is made of fiberglass, metal, plastic, or wood and rests upon the axle and wheels.

Skateboarders have used a variety of sites to showcase their skills. Empty swimming pools and handrails have offered attractive arenas for skateboard enthusiasts.

The Event

Though many tabbed it as a dangerous activity, skateboarding was a featured sport in the opening ceremonies at the 1996 Olympics.

Competitive skateboarding is divided into *downhill*, *slalom*, and *freestyle* formats.

The freestyle event is the most glamorous and dangerous of the three formats. It requires the contestants to perform stunts while riding.

Athletes also perform on large *ramps*. Vertical ramps may be 14 feet (4 meters) or higher. The skateboarder enters one or more of three classes. In *liptricks*, the skater performs tricks around the *coping* of the ramp, or the metal pipe on the ramp's lip. With *inverts*, the athlete skates up, grabs the coping with one hand and the board with the other, then executes a gymnastics-type stunt. In *airs*, skateboarders gain sufficient momentum to jump above the ramp, grab the board, and turn one way or the other.

A few skateboarders are able to earn money through exhibitions and contests. Normally, a skateboard manufacturer sponsors the athlete, and in return he or she uses their product.

History

Skateboarding emerged in California in the early 1960s, when surfing captivated the nation. Surfers enjoyed a sensation similar to riding a wave. In 1965, however, critics charged that the sport was too dangerous and urged stores not to sell skateboards.

The sport reemerged in the 1980s with the introduction of the plywood ramp. Stars such as Tony Hawk, Christian Hosoi, and Steve Caballero developed avid followings among people and gave a cult status to the sport.

Skateboarding received a tremendous boost in 1995 when ESPN included it in its Extreme Games held in Newport, Rhode Island. This introduced the sport to many people who had never before watched skateboarding. It also helped eliminate stereotypes that the activity was not a true sport.

Skateboarding was selected to be a featured sport in the opening ceremonies for the 1996 Olympics. It is currently governed by the International Association of Skateboard Companies.

Skateboarding legend Tony Hawk (black helmet), celebrates after landing a "900"—a 900-degree rotation (two and a half spins)—in mid-air. The trick had never before been accomplished.

Practice Makes Perfect

Tony Hawk has been compared to baseball's immortal Babe Ruth for the impact he has had on his sport. As a teenager, he quickly became the top participant. Today, he remains one of the best competitors. He claims that two characteristics propelled him to excellence—he worked hard to establish the sport with the American public, and he practiced constantly to perfect his moves.

111

Sled Dog Racing

Sled dog racing is the sport of racing sled dog teams across snow. It is popular in Alaska, Canada, and Europe.

Date of Origin	**1908**
Place of Origin	**United States**
Legendary Performer	**Joe Redington, Sr.**
Governing Body	**International Sled Dog Racing Association**
Where They Compete	**Canada, Alaska, Europe**
Championship Events	**Open World Championship Sled Dog Race, Iditarod Sled Dog Race**

Equipment

The wooden *sleds* are between 6 and 13 feet (1.8 to 4 meters) long and 1 and 2 feet (30 to 60 centimeters) wide. The back end has *rails* on which the driver stands and a *bar* for him to grasp. The sleds rest upon wooden or metal *runners*.

The number of dogs on a sled dog team varies from three to ten. Typically, one dog serves as the *lead dog*. Purebred dogs, such as the Siberian husky or the Alaskan malamute, are commonly used, but crossbred dogs are also selected.

Dogs are hooked to a harness and collar. No muzzles or collars hooked as full choke-collars are allowed.

The Event

The most common form of sled dog racing is the *Nome-style racing*, in which dogs are hitched together in teams of two. The driver, or *musher*, stands at the rear and controls the dogs, though he may also run along at the rear from time to time while maintaining hold of the bar. Trained dog teams average close to 20 miles (32 kilometers) per hour. Any dog that becomes ill during the races must be carried in the sled.

Contestants may enter *speed races* that cover a shorter distance, or *long-distance races* that can last 500 to 1,170 miles (800 to 1,900 kilometers). The longer events use up

A six-dog sled race over thirty miles is held in northern New England.

A musher drives his team across the frozen Norton Sound near Nome, Alaska during the Iditarod Trail Sled Dog Race.

to twenty dogs, take days or weeks to complete, and offer rest stops along the way. The most renowned event is the annual Iditarod Sled Dog Race, which runs from Anchorage to Nome, Alaska, a distance of 1,150 miles (1,850 kilometers). Contestants come from many parts of the world to compete in this race.

History

Sled dogs have been used for hundreds of years by people in northern climates for transportation and hunting. In many ways, they are as important as the horse was to inhabitants of the American West. Sled dogs gained fame by taking explorers to the North and South Poles, and many North American youth were familiar with the sight of a Royal Canadian Mounted Police official on his dogsled.

Sled dog racing probably started in Siberia or other snowbound areas in which dog-driven sleds served as a main method of transportation. Nome, Alaska, hosted the first organized sled dog race in 1908.

Female Invasion

No female musher had ever driven her team to victory in the Iditarod race until Libby Riddles broke the barrier in 1985. The following year, another woman, Susan Butcher, set a record finishing time: 11 days, 15 hours, 6 minutes. Butcher won the Iditarod the next two years and claimed four titles in her career.

One of the greatest competitors in this sport is Joe Redington, Sr. An adventurer and lover of the outdoors, he opened a successful Alaskan kennel which produced a string of championship dogs used in sled dog racing. In 1971, he achieved his dream when he successfully organized the first Iditarod race. Since then he has completed nineteen Iditarods, making him a household name in Alaska and Canada.

Snowboarding

Snowboarding is a combination of surfing and skiing. It has drawn many outdoor enthusiasts to snow-covered hills and rises.

Equipment

Snowboards are made of laminated wood over foam centers. They have steel edges for easier turning and navigating through the snow. They are normally about 5 feet (1.5 meters) in length. Bindings hold the *snowboarder's* feet in place.

The Event

Competitive snowboarding involves *freestyle events* and *racing events*. In the *halfpipe competition*, athletes perform stunts in a ditch dug into the snow. The halfpipe stretches 250 to 350 feet (77.5 to 108.5 meters) long with sides that rise anywhere from 7 to 14 feet (2.3 to 4.7 meters) on each side. Snowboarders glide up and down the sides to gain momentum, then execute their tricks before judges.

In *slopestyle competition*, the athlete must navigate a course while doing a series of tricks. For instance, he or she must glide along the top of a downed tree or a metal bar without losing balance.

Judges award points for how well athletes perform their stunts. Each person performs twice, and the winner is the individual who totals the highest number of points.

Racing competition includes the *slalom*, the *giant slalom*, the *parallel slalom*, and the *super G race*. In slalom events, skiers race through a series of *gates* as they speed down the course. The giant slalom uses a steeper slope than the slalom. The parallel slalom pits two skiers racing at the same time. The super G race is held on the steepest of slopes.

Snowboarders have taken traditional ski slopes by storm.

Kim Stacey of the United States catches the lip during the women's World Cup Snowboarding Half Pipe competition at the site of the 2002 Olympics in Utah.

Racers must have both feet on the snowboard when passing a gate. If the racer misses a gate, he or she must return and pass through it before continuing.

Like any athletic activity, snowboarding has a set of rules for recreational participants. Before embarking upon a maneuver, a snowboarder should make sure no one is approaching from behind. In passing a slower person, the snowboarder should yell, "On your left!" Finally, snowboarders should not stop in any area where they can't be seen by people behind them.

History

Snowboarding gained popularity in 1965 when Sherman Poppen bolted together two skis to surf on the snow. He called it the Snurfer. In the early 1970s, an avid snowboarder named Jake Burton perfected the snowboard.

Star on the Slopes

One of the biggest stars in snowboarding is the Mount Vernon, Washington, native Craig Kelly. He first snowboarded at age fifteen, and from that moment on he hit the slopes whenever possible. In 1986 he won the World Slalom Championship, the first of his eventual four world titles and three United States championships. Kelly retired from competitive snowboarding in 1991.

In 1988, the first World Cup of snowboarding was organized by the North American Snowboard Association and the Snowboarding European Association. The World Cup is designed to promote the sport and to determine snowboard champions. Other events in Europe and North America offer financial rewards to top athletes.

With the popularity the sport enjoys, both among participants and television spectators, snowboard enthusiasts hope to add their sport to the Winter Olympics.

Soccer

Date of Origin
1863
Place of Origin
England
Legendary Performers
**Sir Stanley Matthews, Pelé,
Franz Beckenbauer,
Mia Hamm**
Governing Body
**Fédération Internationale
de Football Association**
Where They Compete
Worldwide
Championship Events
**World Cup,
Olympic Games**

Soccer, also known as football, is the world's most popular sport. Many European and Latin American nations consider it their national sport.

Equipment

Soccer is played on a rectangular grass or artificial turf field. It varies in size from 100 to 130 yards (91 to 119 meters) long and from 50 to 100 yards (46 to 91 meters) wide. At each end stands a *goal* consisting of two 8 feet (2.4 meters) high posts that are set 8 yards (7.3 meters) apart. They are connected at the top with a crossbar.

The field is bounded on the side by *touch lines* and on the end by *goal lines*. A *halfway line* divides the playing surface into two equal parts. The *center circle* rests in the middle of the halfway line. A *goal area* 60 feet (18 meters) wide and 18 feet (5.5 meters) deep stretches in front of each goal to offer the *goalkeeper* room to defend his or her goal.

There is a *penalty area* in front of each goal. If the defending team commits a *foul*, the attacking team is awarded a *penalty kick*. This rectangular area is 132 feet (40.2 meters) wide and 54 feet (16.5 meters) deep. The penalty kick line is 36 feet (11.8 meters) from the goal.

The *soccer ball* is made of leather or a similar material. It measures 27 to 28 inches (68 to 71 centimeters) in circumference and weighs from fourteen to sixteen ounces (396 to 453 grams).

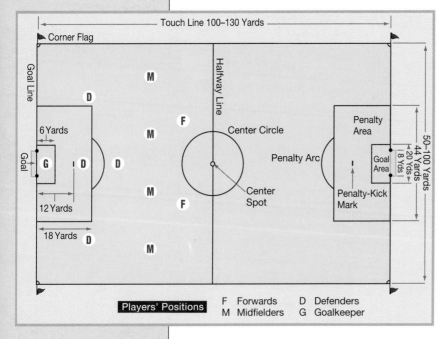

116

Players wear leather shoes with studs or bars, calf-length socks, jerseys with numbers, and shorts. Goalkeepers wear a different color jersey.

The Event

Each team has eleven players. In front of the goalkeeper stand four *defenders*, four *midfielders*, and two *forwards*. The number of each may vary, depending on team strategy.

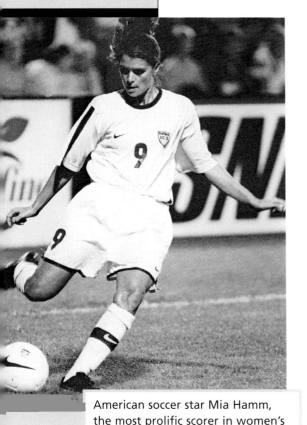

American soccer star Mia Hamm, the most prolific scorer in women's soccer history.

The defenders, also called *fullbacks*, try to prevent the opposing team from getting to the goalkeeper. Midfielders, also called *halfbacks*, assist the defenders and advance the ball to their own forwards when they gain possession. They are expected to contribute on both offense and defense. The forwards, also called *strikers*, attack the opponent's area and try to score goals. They try to score by either kicking the ball on the ground or deflecting an airborne ball with their heads.

The goalkeeper must prevent the other team from kicking or deflecting the ball into their goal. No player except the goalkeeper may use any part of his or her hands or arms.

In international matches only two substitutions are permitted to each team. The player who is removed cannot reenter the game. If the substitution number has been reached and a player is injured, the team may not replace the player.

Games last two *halves* of forty-five minutes each. An intermission of at least five minutes separates the halves. Play begins with the kick-off. Teams advance the ball by dribbling or by passing it to teammates.

When the ball bounces over the side line, a *throw-in* is called. An opponent of the team which last touched the ball tosses the ball back in with both hands in an over-the-head motion.

When the attacking team knocks the ball across the goal line, but outside the goal area, the defending team puts it back into play with a *goal kick*. When the defenders deflect the ball over the goal line, the attacking team uses a *corner kick* to put the ball back into play.

A goal is scored when one team knocks the ball beyond the opposing goalkeeper and into the goal. The team that scores the most goals wins. In the event of a tie, the game may be decided either with extra playing time or with penalty kicks.

A *free kick* is granted to a team when the referee calls a foul (offsides, tripping, holding) on the opponent. The kick is taken at the spot where the violation occurred. Members of the other team must move at least 10 yards (9 meters) away.

Major fouls committed by the defending team inside their penalty area results in a *penalty kick*. A member of the attacking team places the ball on the penalty line. Only the goaltender may try to stop the kick.

History

The earliest form of soccer occurred in ancient China. The emperor Huang-ti started a game in 1697 B.C. called *tsu-chu*. The Japanese followed with their own version one thousand years later.

Ancient Greeks and Romans also had versions of soccer. Wherever Roman legionnaires were

Brazil's Pelé is soccer's greatest ambassador. His talents and accomplishments are legendary.

stationed throughout Europe, they introduced one of their favorite pastimes, a game called *harpastum*. English citizens particularly loved the rough format and developed a contest called the *ludus pilae*, which eventually used leather-covered balls. The men and boys from one English village frequently challenged the men and boys of another, and the winner in this no-holds-barred contest was the team that batted the ball into the opposing village.

The game spread to English schools in the 1800s. In 1848, a group of athletes from Cambridge University compiled a set of rules. Fourteen years later, J.C. Thring revised them and they were adopted by the London Football Association on December 8, 1863. Modern soccer was born.

Soccer gradually spread to other parts of Europe, the British Empire, and to the Americas. People in Europe and South America often elevate a soccer match against a rival nation to the proportions of a national event. Victory earns nationwide praise, while defeat brings disgrace to the team.

In 1904, the governing body of soccer, the Fédération Internationale de Football Association, was formed. Under its guidance, soccer has become the world's number one sport. The game's premier event, the World Cup, brings together teams from nations around the world every four years to determine a world champion.

France won its first-ever World Cup in 1998. They stunned Brazil by defeating them 3-0 in the championship game. With four world championships, Brazil holds the most world titles by a country. Italy and Germany have won the championship three times each.

The Greatest Ever

Soccer did not enjoy widespread popularity in the United States until the arrival of the game's most revered player, Pelé. A national hero in Brazil, Pelé played professional soccer in the United States in the mid-1970s. His efforts helped popularize soccer in the United States.

119

Softball

Softball is a sport in which a team tries to score more runs than its opponent. The sport is very popular in the United States.

Equipment

Softball's playing field consists of an *infield* and an *outfield*. *Bases* are placed 60 feet (18.3 meters) from one another to form a diamond shape. The *pitcher's mound* stands 46 feet (14 meters) from *home plate*. White *foul lines* extend from home plate's apex to the outfield. They divide the playing field into *fair territory* and *foul territory*.

The regulation *softball* is 12 inches (30.5 centimeters) in circumference. *Bats* are between 26 and 33 inches (66 and 84 centimeters) in length and weigh from 20 to 24 ounces (560 to 672 grams).

The Event

A regulation softball contest lasts seven *innings*. Each team takes a turn at bat and in the field to complete an inning. The team at bat has three *outs*. A *run* is scored each time a player safely touches each base before the third out is registered.

The *pitcher* throws the ball underhanded. In *fast-pitch softball*, the pitcher throws the ball hard, while in *slow-pitch softball*, the ball is lobbed to the plate. Four *infielders* and three *outfielders* support the pitcher. In slow-pitch softball, four outfielders are used.

The first athlete steps inside the *batter's box* and waits for the ball to be delivered from the opposing pitcher. A *strike* is called if the *batter* swings and misses, if he or she hits the ball but it lands in foul territory, or if he or she does not swing but the pitch passes through the *strike zone* (the area over home plate

The windmill delivery is the most popular method of pitching in women's fast-pitch softball.

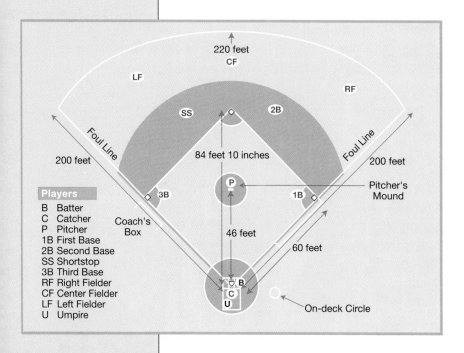

Players

B   Batter
C   Catcher
P   Pitcher
1B First Base
2B Second Base
SS Shortstop
3B Third Base
RF Right Fielder
CF Center Fielder
LF Left Fielder
U   Umpire

between the batter's knees and armpits). After a third strike, the batter is called *out* and the next player steps up to bat. If the batter does not swing at a pitch, and the pitch fails to pass through the strike zone, the umpire calls a *ball*. With the fourth ball, the player is sent to *first base*.

A player registers a *hit* when he or she bats the ball into fair territory and it touches the ground before a defending player catches it, or if the batter reaches first base before a defender throws the ball to the *first baseman*. The batter may continue running beyond first base, but he or she is called out if tagged by a player holding the ball.

The team at bat tries to score as many runs as possible before the third out. The team with the highest run total after seven innings wins. If the teams are tied, they play extra innings until one outscores the other.

History

In 1887, G. W. Handcock of Chicago, Illinois, created softball as an indoor version of baseball. Eight years later, Lewis Rober produced the outdoor form in Minneapolis, Minnesota, with slightly different rules. In 1968, the United States Slow-Pitch Softball Association (USSSA) was formed to govern the game's rapid growth. More than forty million people in the United States play softball.

A Golden Birth

Women's fast-pitch softball finally became an official Olympic sport in 1996. The U.S. team won a gold medal.

121

Speed Skating

Speed skating requires strength, endurance, and quickness. Because it is performed on ice, balance and technique are also important.

Equipment

The long, narrow blades help speed skaters attain speeds of 35 miles (56 kilometers) per hour. The steel blade measures 12 to 18 inches (30 to 45 centimeters) long and .03 inch (0.8 millimeter) wide. Speed skaters wear gloves and a lightweight, tight-fitting uniform that is customized to reduce wind friction.

The Event

Speed skaters compete in one of four different types of races. In *pack style skating*, a group of skaters line up at designated starting positions and attempt to be the first to cross the finish line. Pack skating meets are usually held on tracks that measure 437 yards (400 meters) around.

Long track skating features two skaters competing against each other on a two-lane track. Distances range from 500 to 10,000 meters. Long track skating is most widely used in the Olympic Games and in international meets.

Short track skating events feature two types of races—*individual races* and *relay races*. In the first, individual skaters compete in distances of either 500, 1,000, 1,500, or 3,000 meters (547, 1,094, 1,640, 3,280 yards). Relay races pit two four-member teams against each other.

Marathon racing tests endurance and stamina. Athletes race on courses of either 25 or 50 kilometers. Although races are very competitive, marathon racing is not an Olympic event.

Strong legs and balance allow the best skaters to lead the pack.

Longer races (such as the 5,000-meter race) require excellent form, strength, and stamina.

Skaters must use swift, clean starts, proper form, powerful leg thrusts, and long, smooth arm strokes. The skater's technique varies slightly according to the race's length. For all races, skaters lean forward at the waist, with knees bent, head up, and eyes staring straight ahead. In races up to 1,500 meters (1,640 yards), athletes use the two-arm swing, alternating arms with each leg stroke. For longer races, they switch to the one-arm swing, in which they tuck one arm behind their backs while swinging with the other. They may also clutch both arms behind their backs on straightaways.

History

In the 16th century, Holland's frozen canals and waterways held some of the first speed races. The sport spread to England, where racing matches occurred as early as 1814.

Norwegian speed skaters monopolized international racing until the 1920s. In 1924, male speed skating was added to the Olympic Games, and female speed skating followed in 1960. Today, American, Russian, and Scandinavian athletes excel on the ice. In the United States, the sport is governed by the Amateur Skating Union of the United States.

Good as Gold

In the 1980 Olympic Games, American skater Eric Heiden compiled one of the sport's most heralded records. Not only did he become the first athlete to win all five of the speed skating events, but he established new records in each of the five.

The sport became popular in the United States when a famed speed-skating family revolutionized skating. T. Donoghue and his two sons attached a longer blade to the boot, then combined the innovation with a shorter leg stroke. The Donoghues dominated the sport and established numerous records in their time.

Squash

Squash, or squash racquets, is an indoor game in which a hard, hollow rubber ball is hit against walls with a mesh racquet. The game is popular in Europe, the United States, Canada, and Mexico.

Equipment

The dimensions for an American *squash court* for singles competition is 18.5 feet (5.6 meters) wide and 32 feet (9.7 meters) long. The court for doubles competition is slightly larger. A *service line* runs 6.5 feet (2 meters) above the floor and marks the lowest point where the opening volley, called the *service*, may be hit. To begin play, the *server* must stand behind the *service-court line*, which is 18 feet (5.5 meters) from the front wall.

The circular-headed racquet may have a diameter no larger than 9 inches (22.9 centimeters), and the racquet's length may not exceed 27 inches (68 centimeters). The racquet is strung with a nylon or catgut mesh.

The Event

The server starts the game by hitting the ball from behind the service-court line. The ball must hit above the service line on the front wall and bounce on the fly into the opponent's service area. The server has two chances to successfully land a serve. Should he or she fail on both attempts, the opponent gets to serve.

After a successful service, the opponent must hit the ball before it bounces twice with sufficient impact to reach the front wall above the *telltale*—a line on the front wall 2 feet

Quick feet and accurate shooting are skills that good squash players possess.

Beast of the East

Though popular along the East Coast in the United States, squash is a hard sport to find out West. Most tournaments began in the East. In 1911 the National Squash Association held its first tournament in New York City. Greenwich, Connecticut, hosted the first women's championship, and many early stars emerged from eastern states.

(.6 meters) above the floor. The server then does likewise, and the players volley until one fails to return the ball to the front wall, hits the ball below the telltale, or hits it above a play line extending around the court 16 feet (4.9 meters) high from the front wall to the service line and 12 feet (3.7 meters) from there to the back wall.

The server continues to serve until he or she loses a volley, at which time the opponent serves. In international competition only the server receives points, while in American play both the server and receiver earn points. The game ends at fifteen points in American play and at nine under English rules.

History

Squash evolved from an earlier game played in England called racquets.

It is said that as students of the Harrow's School in England waited to play the game on the school's sole racquets court, they batted another ball around in a much smaller area nearby. Because of the cramped space, they used a softer ball which could be "squashed" in one's hand, thus giving rise to the new game.

As students graduated from Harrow, they introduced the newer format throughout the nation. The sport found a home among the wealthy, who constructed courts on their estates.

The game appeared in the United States in 1882, where it became a favorite in high schools, colleges, and athletic clubs. The U.S. Squash Racquets Association governs the sport in the United States, which held its first national championship in squash in 1907. The game, in both the hardball and softball format, has exploded in popularity since the end of World War II in 1945.

Surfing

Surfing, the sport of riding waves on a floating device called a *surfboard*, has captivated millions of people around the world. The *surfer* attempts to remain upright on a wave as it rushes toward shore.

Equipment

Surfing is popular because all one needs is a body of water and a surfboard. Once made of a heavy wood, boards are now made of lightweight balsa wood or fiberglass. Many are covered with paraffin wax to help reduce slipping.

Surfboards under 7 feet (2 meters) long are called *shortboards*, and those over 7 feet are called *longboards*. The boards gently slope down from either tip to the middle, and a fin underneath helps balance the board.

The Event

A surfer paddles out on his board from the beach to the point where the waves first break. The surfer then waits face-down on his board until a desirable wave approaches. He then begins to paddle toward shore. As the wave advances underneath the board and edges it along, the surfer stands up. If he has timed the move properly, he will be rushing on his board toward shore, propelled by the *face* of the wave, the smooth wall of water directly below the wave's crest. He can steer the board by moving his rear foot to the right or left while keeping his other foot in the center of the board. For a longer ride, the surfer tries to stay close to the face of the wave and surf in the direction the wave is traveling.

Surfing demands precise timing and quick reflexes, which enable the participant to hit the

Surfing requires great balance and body control.

126

wave at exactly the right moment and take full advantage of its momentum. Experienced surfers stand closer to the board's front, where balance is more difficult to maintain. Some participants enjoy performing acrobatic skills while riding a wave, such as circular turns on the wave's face or riding up and down the wave.

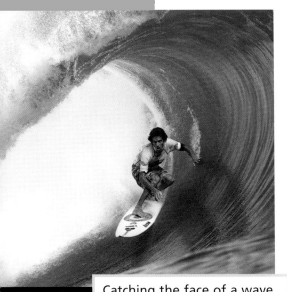

Catching the face of a wave is an indescribable rush for surfers.

History

Noted Pacific Ocean explorer Captain James Cook found native Hawaiians engaging in surfing when he first arrived in the islands in 1778. Practiced as a form of religious ceremony, Hawaiian nobility used huge surfboards that weighed as much as 150 pounds (68 kilograms) and stretched 18 feet (5.4 meters) long. European missionaries tried to eliminate the sport because they thought it was a "pagan" practice, but surfing maintained its hold.

The sport appeared in the United States and Australia in the early 1900s, but grew slowly because of the weight of the boards. In 1920, a Hawaiian Olympic swimming champion, Duke Kahanamoku, formed the first surfing club. When Kahanamoku visited the mainland United States, observers quickly took to the sport. When smaller, lighter boards came into use in the 1940s, surfing became even more accessible. In the 1960s, a musical group called The Beach Boys helped popularize the sport outside California, where it was common by then.

Captain Cook

The famed English explorer Captain Cook observed Hawaiian surfing during his 1778 visit to the islands. He commented in his diary that despite the dangers of being crashed against the rocks, the natives willingly "place themselves on the summit of the largest surge, by which they are driven along with amazing rapidity toward the shore."

All forms of surfing, including amateur and professional levels, are governed by the International Council of Associations of Surfing.

Swimming

Swimming is the art of moving the body through water by using the arms and legs. While it has emerged as a highly competitive sport, swimming is also one of the best forms of recreational activities and rehabilitation from injuries.

Equipment

The Fédération Internationale de Natation Amateur (FINA) ensures that regulations are followed in international *swim meets*. Meets are held in either *long-course pools*, which measure 164 feet (50 meters) long, or *short-course pools* half the size. The pool contains six to ten swimming *lanes*, each about 8 feet (2.4 meters) wide. Water must be at least 4 feet (1.2 meters) deep and have a temperature of 78°F (26°C).

Swimming has five main strokes—the *crawl*, the *backstroke*, the *breaststroke*, the *butterfly*, and the *sidestroke*. Each stroke is unique and requires the use of different body parts and muscle regions. Speed and strength are instrumental to swimmers, but technique may be the most important factor in competitive swimming. Good form allows the swimmer to maximize his or her strength and overall potential.

The Event

Individual swimmers compete in five races—*freestyle,* breaststroke, backstroke, butterfly, and a combination of the four called the *individual medley*. Most races are held at distances ranging from 100 to 1,500 meters (109 to 1,640 yards). Swim meets also offer four-member team relays, in which the swimmers each swim an equal distance.

Each swimmer receives a lane. At the sound of the starter's gun, the swimmers push off or leap into the water, turn at the

In the backstroke event, swimmers begin in the water and dive back when the starting gun sounds.

128

other end, and repeat the process until the required number of lengths are completed. Plates attached to the pool's end record each contestant's time as the swimmer's hand touches it.

Synchronized swimming combines the grace of ballet with coordination. This event requires an individual or a team of swimmers to perform a series of movements to music.

History

Swimming is found in the records of many ancient civilizations, including Egypt, Greece, and Rome. The activity declined during the Middle Ages (A.D. 500 to 1500) because people thought that the plague and other fatal diseases were spread by water.

Olympic gold medalist Tracy Caulkins performs the breaststroke during the individual medley event.

Swimming reappeared in the 1800s, both as a recreational activity and as a competition. At first a technique called the *Australian crawl* dominated freestyle swimming, but an American swimmer named Johnny Weissmuller adapted the stroke to what is now the front crawl. He later set more than sixty-five world records and won five gold medals in the 1924 and 1928 Olympic Games.

Johnny Be Good

American swimmer Johnny Weissmuller set numerous swimming records during his career. He was the first athlete to shatter the one-minute mark in the 100-meter event. After he retired, Weissmuller became an actor. He was one of the first on-screen Tarzans, and his voice was used for Tarzan's yell in later movies.

Other famous swimmers include Mark Spitz, who stunned the sports world by capturing seven gold medals in the 1972 Olympics; Matt Biondi, who won seven medals in the 1988 Olympic Games; and Dawn Fraser, an Australian who set numerous women's marks, including gold medals in the freestyle event in three successive Olympics.

129

Table Tennis

More commonly known as Ping Pong, table tennis is an indoor variation of lawn tennis played on a table with a small ball and rackets, called *paddles*. In parts of Asia, table tennis is a major sport.

Equipment

The table measures 9 feet (2.7 meters) long by 5 feet (1.5 meters) wide, with a playing surface 30 inches (76 centimeters) above the floor. The surface bears a white line along the edges as a border and a white *center line* running lengthwise, which divides the table into four sections called *courts*. A mesh *net* 6 inches (15 centimeters) high stretches across the table's center and overlaps the edges 6 inches on each side.

The paddles vary in size, weight, and shape, but generally contain a striking surface of 6 to 7 inches (15 to 17 centimeters) in diameter with handles 3 to 4 inches (7 to 10 centimeters) long. The wooden paddles are covered with a pimpled or smooth surface of rubber extended across a thin layer of sponge rubber. The hollow ball, 1.5 inches (3.8 centimeters) in diameter and weighing about .10 ounces, is made from celluloid or plastic.

The Event

The object in table tennis is to score points by hitting the ball so that the opponent cannot return it. The first player (or two-man team) to reach twenty-one points wins the match. If the score is tied at twenty, the first player to achieve a two-point lead wins the game.

Play starts when the *server* strikes the ball with his paddle. The ball must bounce once in the server's half of the table before crossing the net, at which time the opponent waits for the

The server flips the ball to himself to strike his serve.

ball to bounce once on his or her side before hitting it back. The ball is hit back and forth, always after one bounce, until someone fails to return the ball to the opponent's side. Service is switched after every five serves.

In doubles matches, the player who is serving must hit the ball from his or her right-hand court across the net into the opponents' right-hand court. From then on, teams alternate returning the ball.

History

Table tennis is believed to have originated in London, England, in the early 1880s. In 1900, the current celluloid ball replaced the cork variety. Because of the peculiar sound which the celluloid ball made—a "ping" when it hit the paddle, a "pong" when it hit the table—the game came to be known as Ping Pong.

In 1921, a group of players began calling the game table tennis, and five years later the International Table Tennis Federation appeared. It offered the sport's first world championships that year, held in London. In 1933, the U.S. Table Tennis Association became the governing body for American tournaments. The game became an Olympic sport in 1988.

In the 1970s, table tennis helped improve diplomatic relations between the United States and China, which had been severed since 1949. First an American table tennis team toured the Asian nation in a series of exhibitions against the Chinese team. Then President Richard M. Nixon announced that he would visit China the next year. His successful journey to China in 1972, prepared in part through what had become known as "ping-pong diplomacy," opened new areas of agreement between the two nations.

Tennis

Tennis is an indoor or outdoor sport in which either two or four players use a *racket* to hit a ball back and forth across a net. Tennis is played in practically every nation in the world.

Origin
1873
Place of Origin
England
Legendary Performers
William Tilden II,
Billie Jean King, Bjorn Borg,
Chris Evert Lloyd,
Pete Sampras,
Governing Body
International Tennis
Federation
Where They Compete
Worldwide
Championship Events
Davis Cup, Wimbledon,
U.S. Open, French Open,
Australian Open

Equipment

The rectangular *tennis court* measures 78 feet (23 meters) long and 27 feet (8.2 meters) wide for singles or 36 feet (11 meters) wide for doubles. A mesh net 3 feet (90 centimeters) high in the middle and 3 feet 6 inches (105 centimeters) at the ends divides the court in half, while white markings split the court into singles and doubles sections. Courts consist either of grass, asphalt, clay, or concrete surfaces.

The *tennis ball* is a hollow rubber sphere covered with a felt fabric made of Dacron, nylon, and wool. It measures between 2.5 inches and 2.6 inches (6.3 to 6.6 centimeters) in diameter, and must weigh between 2 ounces and 2.16 ounces (57 to 58.4 grams).

The racket is about 27 inches (68 centimeters) long. The oval head of the racket is strung with catgut or nylon string. A *handgrip* of rubber or other material covers the handle.

The Event

The game starts with one player serving. The ball must pass over the net and land in the opposite service court. The opponent then attempts to hit the ball back. The volley continues until one side fails to return the ball across the net or into the playing area.

Each *game* consists of four points—scored *fifteen, thirty, forty, game*—unless a tie occurs. If the game is tied at forty, called *deuce*, the

Anna Kournikova reaches to hit her return shot.

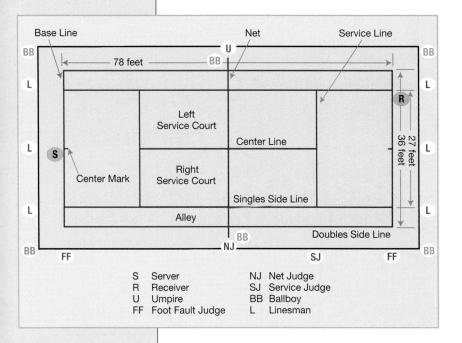

S	Server	NJ	Net Judge
R	Receiver	SJ	Service Judge
U	Umpire	BB	Ballboy
FF	Foot Fault Judge	L	Linesman

game continues until one player wins by two points. The first player to win six games wins a *set*. However, if competitors are tied at five games apiece, the victor must go ahead by two games (7-5) to win the set. If they're deadlocked at six games, one final game is played to determine the set. Tennis *matches* consist of the best of three sets for women and the best of five for men.

History

In 1873, England's Major Walter Clopton Wingfield introduced a game similar to modern lawn tennis. Four years later, England sponsored the first lawn tennis championship.

Lawn tennis quickly spread to Europe and the United States, which held its first U.S. Open in 1881. That tournament, combined with Wimbledon, the French Open, and the Australian Open, form tennis's "Grand Slam."

In the United States, William T. "Big Bill" Tilden II popularized the sport in the 1920s. In the 1970s and 1980s, Americans Jimmy Connors and John McEnroe battled Swedish sensation Bjorn Borg, while Americans Billie Jean King and Chris Evert Lloyd battled Martina Navratilova. In more recent years, Pete Sampras of the United States and Germany's Steffi Graf dominated tournament play.

Chris Evert Lloyd

Hall of Fame tennis player Chris Evert Lloyd played best in the big tournaments. Throughout her career, she won 90 percent of her matches. Among her 157 victories are eighteen Grand Slam titles—three Wimbledon victories, seven French Open championships, six U.S. Open titles, and two Australian Open crowns.

Track & Field

The decathlon is one of two combined events in track and field (the other is the heptathlon). *Deca-* means "ten," and in the decathlon male athletes compete in ten different events over a period of two days.

Equipment

Participants in the decathlon use the entire track and field area in the course of their competition. Like all athletes in track and field, they wear lightweight shorts, a jersey, and special track shoes.

The Event

Athletes participate in five events each day. The first day's schedule starts with the *100-meter dash*, then follows with the *long jump*, the *shot put*, the *high jump*, and the *400-meter dash*. On the second day athletes begin with the *110-meter hurdles*, then compete in the *discus*, the *pole vault*, the *javelin throw*, and end with the *1500-meter run*.

German decathlete David Mewes shows his intensity during the shot put part of the decathlon.

Athletes are given at least thirty minutes rest between the end of one event and the start of another. Rules follow the normal procedure for each individual event, except that the athletes are permitted only three attempts in the jumping and throwing events, and they are disqualified from the decathlon if they incur two false starts in any event.

The winner is the athlete who compiles the highest number of points over the two days. If there is a tie, the contestant who attained the highest point total in the most events is declared the winner. If the tie persists, the athlete who achieved the highest single point total in any one of the events is the victor.

History

To many, decathlon participants are the best athletes in the world. They combine strength, speed, endurance, and leaping ability.

Variations on the decathlon have existed for years, but the event that is included in the Olympics today first appeared in 1912. The United States has had great success in the decathlon through the years, including victories by Jim Thorpe in 1912, Bob Mathias in 1948 and 1952, Rafer Johnson in 1960, Bruce Jenner in 1976, and Dan O'Brien in 1996.

Mathias amazed onlookers for two reasons—his pure athletic talent and his youth. At the suggestion of his coach, the seventeen-year-old entered his first decathlon, the Southern Pacific AAU Games in Los Angeles, with only three weeks to prepare. Mathias had never participated in a decathlon—football and basketball were his games. He surprised everyone by winning the event.

When he traveled to London, England, for the 1948 Olympic Games, the youthful Mathias received little consideration by experts. However, he again stunned the track and field world by winning the Olympic gold medal in only his third decathlon.

Bruce Jenner captured the 1976 gold medal in Montreal. After finishing tenth in the 1972 Olympic Games, Jenner set a world decathlon record in 1976.

Dan O'Brien has excelled in the decathlon for most of the 1990s. He holds the world record with a mark of 8,891 points and the Olympic record with 8,824 points.

Young Gun

Winning one Olympic decathlon earns admiration from the entire track and field world because of the immense talent, tireless effort, and hard work required. Bob Mathias gained distinction in 1948 by becoming the youngest to ever win a decathlon. However, four years later he topped that by winning another decathlon to become the first athlete ever to win successive Olympic decathlons.

135

Track & Field

Discus is a field event in which men and women hurl a heavy disc from inside a circled area to a field.

Equipment

The *discus* is a saucer-shaped piece of wood or other material that has a weighted center and a metal rim. The men's discus weighs at least 4 pounds 6.5 ounces (2 kilograms). The women's discus weighs at least 2 pounds 3 ounces (1 kilogram).

The athlete throws the discus from a *circle* 8 feet 2.5 inches (2.5 meters) in diameter. Two *sector lines* form a 40-degree angle within which the discus must be thrown.

The Event

A competitor starts in a stationary position with his back to the field. The discus may be thrown in any manner, as long as the athlete remains inside the circle during the throw. The discus must land within the marked field.

If the event has eight or fewer contestants, each individual receives six throws, called *trials*. For competitions with more than eight, each has three throws, and the top eight individuals then receive three additional tosses. Throws are measured from the nearest mark made on the field by the discus to the circle's inner edge. The athlete with the longest throw wins the competition.

The ancient Greeks revered discus champions. The event is mentioned in the writings of Homer, and it first appeared in the Olympics in 708 B.C.

Strength and technique are equally important to throwing the discus great distances.

Track & Field

The hammer throw is a field event in which a heavy ball on a chain is tossed from a caged area into a field.

Equipment

The *hammer* weighs 16 pounds (7.26 kilograms). The metal *head*, a solid ball, is attached to the 4-foot (1.215-meter) long steel wire. The end of the wire contains a single or double metal loop called the *grip*. This is where the athlete grasps the hammer.

The athlete throws from a *circle* 7 feet (2.14 meters) in diameter. Two white lines called *sector lines* extend from the circle into the field at a 40-degree angle within which the hammer must be thrown.

The Event

The legs and torso play major roles in tossing the hammer.

In tossing the hammer, the competitor begins in a set position with his back to the field and the hammer's head resting on the ground. He holds the grips with both hands and takes two preliminary turns without moving the head. He then twists in three complete turns while swinging the hammer and advancing toward the circle's front. He lets go before stepping on the front line.

Each athlete receives six attempts. The throw is measured from the nearest mark made by the hammer back to the circle's inside edge.

Athletes from the British Isles have thrown the hammer since the 1500s. The event probably started in the Scottish Highland Games, which are said to have been organized by a local ruler who wanted the men in his area to be more physically fit.

Track & Field

The heptathlon is one of two combined events in track and field (the other is the decathlon). Over a period of two days, athletes compete in seven different events.

Equipment

Participants use the entire track and field area in the course of their competition. They wear a lightweight shorts, a jersey, and special track shoes.

The Event

The first day begins with the *100-meter dash*, then follows with the *high jump*, the *shot put*, and the *200-meter dash*. On the second day competitors begin with the *long jump*, then the *javelin* throw, and end with the *800-meter run*.

Athletes are given at least thirty minutes rest between the end of one event and the start of another. The order in which they compete is decided by a drawing before each event. Rules follow the normal format for each individual event, except that athletes are permitted only three attempts in the jumping and throwing events.

The winner is the athlete who compiles the highest number of points over the two days. If there is a tie, the contestant who attained the highest point total in the most events is declared the winner. If the tie persists, the performer who achieved the highest single point total in any one of the events is the victor.

Jackie Joyner-Kersee narrowly clears the bar during the high jump event of the heptathlon.

The heptathlon replaced the *pentathlon* (five events) in 1981.

Track & Field

The high jump is an event in which athletes try to leap over a bar resting atop two uprights.

Date of Origin
1800s
Place of Origin
England
Legendary Performers
Dick Fosbury,
Javier Sotomayor
Governing Body
International Amateur
Athletic Federation
Where They Compete
Worldwide
Championship Events
World Championships,
Olympic Games

Equipment

A fan-shaped *runway* stands in front of the jump area. The runway must extend at least 66 feet (20 meters) from the crossbar. Two *uprights* 13 feet 3 inches (4 meters) apart support the *crossbar*, a round wood or metal rod with flat ends. It must be set so that any slight jar from the athlete knocks it off.

The Event

The athlete approaches the crossbar from any direction. He or she must take off from one foot, and they may cross over the bar with their chest facing upwards or facing downwards.

The competitors receive three jumps. Every athlete who successfully leaps at the height moves to the next round. If an athlete misses with the first jump, he or she may pass on the second and third attempts and wait until the next round. However, three consecutive misses eliminates the competitor.

Athletes use two different forms of jumping over the crossbar. With the *straddle* form, the athlete takes off from the foot nearest the bar, swings the other foot upward and over the bar, and crosses with his or her stomach facing downward. In the *flop* technique, the competitor leaps head first and crosses with the back facing downwards.

Javier Sotomayor of Cuba holds the current world record with a leap of 8 feet 0.5 inches (24.4 meters) in 1993.

A Michigan University student clears 5' 7.75" in the high jump competition during the Big 10 Outdoor Championships.

Track & Field

The javelin is a field event in which the athlete hurls a thin metal shaft as far as possible.

Equipment

The javelin is a metal rod with a *grip* on one end. The javelin used by men is 8 feet 10 inches (2.7 meters) long and weighs 1.8 pounds (800 grams). Women use a javelin that is 7 feet 6 inches (2.3 meters) long and weighs 1.3 pounds (600 grams).

A *runway* stretches 36 to 44 yards (30 to 36.5 meters) long and 13 feet (4 meters) wide. *Sector lines* extend from a point 26 feet 3 inches (8 meters) behind the *running line*.

The Event

Each athlete must clutch the javelin with one hand, at its grip. Competitors must throw it over their shoulder or upper part of the arm. The athletes must always face the direction they are throwing. They may not twist their bodies or place their backs to the arc in an effort to gain momentum. The metallic *tip* of the javelin must hit the ground before any other part of it strikes, and it must land within the sector lines. The athlete may not leave the runway until his or her javelin has touched the ground.

Jan Zalezny of the Czech Republic set the world record in 1996 with a throw of 323 feet, 1 inch (98 meters).

A form of the javelin has been in existence since ancient times. Soldiers competed against one another in throwing their spears. The sport is now governed by the International Amateur Athletic Federation.

Legendary athlete Babe Didrikson Zaharias rears back to toss the javelin.

Track & Field

The long jump is an event in which athletes take a running start and jump as far as they can. It is a very popular Olympic event.

Equipment

Most long jump *runways* are 148 feet (45 meters) long and 4 feet (1.22 meters) wide. At the end of the runway is an 8-inch (20-centimeter) wide white wooden board called the *takeoff board*. An *indicator board* stands immediately beyond the takeoff board and indicates whether the athlete stepped beyond the *takeoff line*. The landing area, or *pit*, is an area of slightly-moistened sand 9 feet 9 inches (3 meters) wide and 29 feet 6 inches (9 meters) long.

Athletes wear the typical lightweight outfit of shorts and a shirt. For better traction, they use spiked shoes.

The Event

If eight or fewer athletes compete in this event, each receives six jumps. If more than eight enter, each receives three jumps, and the eight competitors with the longest jumps receive three additional jumps. The winner is the athlete who records the longest jump. If two or more athletes record the same distance, the winner is the one among them with the next-best jump.

Jesse Owens won four gold medals in the 1936 Olympics, including the long jump event.

Each attempt is measured by officials from the take-off line to the nearest mark, called a *break*, made in the sand by any body part. A jump is ruled illegal if the athlete touches the indicator board, jumps from outside the takeoff board, walks back through the pit, or while landing touches the ground outside the pit behind the break.

Jesse Owens set the Olympic record in the long jump in 1936. He kept it for 24 years until Ralph Boston broke it at the 1960 Olympics.

Track & Field

The marathon is an individual long-distance running event. It is the longest distance running event in track and field and requires extreme training. In recent years, marathon races have included a division for wheelchair athletes, who gain the admiration of spectators and fellow performers for their athleticism and determination.

Date of Origin
490 B.C.
Place of Origin
Greece
Legendary Performers
Emil Zátopek,
Jean Driscoll, Bill Rodgers,
Alberto Salazar,
Grete Waitz,
Joan Samuelson
Governing Bodies
International Amateur
Athletic Federation,
Amateur Athletic Union,
U.S.A. Track and Field
Where They Compete
Worldwide
Championship Events
Olympic Games,
Boston Marathon,
New York City Marathon

Equipment

The marathon can be laid out almost anywhere, as long as there is sufficient room for its length of 26 miles 385 yards (42.195 kilometers). It must not take place on grass or soft turf. The Boston Marathon, for example, winds through city streets and outlying roads before ending in a difficult uphill run.

To gain as much uniformity as possible, most marathons are now laid out in an "out-and-back" format rather than a single direction. This prevents competitors' being aided or hampered throughout the entire race by strong winds.

The Event

Competitors bunch up at the starting line and, at the sound of the gun, proceed to run. Most use the first portion of the race to settle into a steady rhythm. A runner may be disqualified if he or she fails to follow the proper course, or if the person takes refreshments at any place other than the refreshment stations.

Marathon runners wear a look of determination.

Since no two marathon courses are alike, the International Amateur Athletic Federation does not recognize a world record in this event. Each meet keeps its own records, including the Olympic Games.

History

The marathon has one of the most stirring origins of any sporting event. In 490 B.C., the mighty Persian king Darius the Great, anxious to defeat the upstart Greek city-states and punish them for helping his enemies in an earlier war, sent twenty-five thousand well-drilled soldiers to Greece. Ships transported the Persian army across the Aegean Sea and landed them at a place called Marathon.

Bill Rodgers helped popularize marathon running in the 1970s and 1980s.

The twenty-five thousand men found ten-thousand soldiers from Athens waiting for them. Though outnumbered more than two to one, the Athenians charged their surprised opponent, fought in efficient groupings called phalanxes, and defeated them.

According to the traditional story, the Athenian commander ordered a young soldier, Pheidippides, to race back to Athens with word of the victory. Pheidippides ran at top speed for most of the approximately 26-mile distance from Marathon to Athens, gasped "Rejoice, we conquer," and died. The race is named a marathon in memory of this event.

Emil Zátopek

Most marathon runners focus only on that race because of its physical and mental strain. However, in the 1952 Olympic Games a Czechoslovakian runner, Emil Zátopek, won gold medals not only in the marathon but in the 5,000-meter and 10,000-meter races. The triple feat made Zátopek a national hero.

While the Olympic Games continue to be the premier event in marathon racing, other marathons have grown in importance. The annual Boston Marathon draws a top field, including wheelchair entrants like Jean Driscoll, who won the race seven years in a row. New York City and Los Angeles also sponsor important marathons. They are more popular than ever for recreational runners. In 1999, sixty-five thousand runners requested entrance to the New York City marathon.

Track & Field

The pole vault is a field event in which an athlete uses a flexible *pole* to leap over a *crossbar* supported by two *uprights* without knocking it off. The winner is the contestant who successfully leaps the highest.

Equipment

A *runway* leads the athlete to the launching area. Most are 148 feet (45 meters) long. At the end of the runway is the *box*. It's an all-metal or metal-covered wooden area in which the athlete places the pole. Uprights, two metal posts set 14 feet (4.3 meters) apart, support the crossbar. The *landing pit*, 16 feet 5 inches (5 meters) square, is padded for the athlete's protection.

The pole usually weighs at least 4.4 pounds (2 kilograms) and is approximately 16 feet (4.9 meters) long. The pole bends during the vault. Modern poles are made of fiberglass. This provides greater flexibility to catapult higher distances.

Athletes wear lightweight shorts and tops. To gain extra speed and traction, they use spiked shoes.

The Event

Judges announce at which height the bar will be placed to begin the competition. Each competitor decides whether to jump at the announced height or to pass until a later round.

The athlete sprints down the runway with pole in hand and inserts the end of the pole into the box. As the competitor lifts up and clears the crossbar, he or she shoves the pole away so it does not knock off the bar.

An athlete is given three attempts to clear the announced height, or be eliminated. Rounds

Dan O'Brien in mid-approach during the 1996 Summer Olympic Games in Atlanta.

continue at increased heights until only one athlete remains. If the final competitors are eliminated at equal heights (a tie), the contestant with the fewest total misses is named winner.

History

Pole vaulting originated in the medieval English custom of using a pole to jump streams or marshy areas. This led to contests in which men jumped for distance rather than for height. Competitive pole vaulting for height started in the mid-nineteenth century, when Englishmen used wooden poles containing spikes to jump over obstacles.

Pole vaulting is now a fixture at national, international, and Olympic meets. In the United States, the event has gained popularity through the efforts of the Amateur Athletic Union (AAU). The AAU, organized in 1888, sponsors meets throughout the nation and hosts instructional forums for young athletes.

For years, American athletes dominated the sport. From 1896 through 1968, pole vaulters from the United States won sixteen of seventeen gold medals at the Olympic Games. John Velses, a twenty-four-year-old Marine corporal, was the first to vault more than 16 feet (48.7 meters).

On July 31, 1994, Sergey Bubka of the Ukraine set a new world record by vaulting 20 feet 1.75 inches. That vault still holds its place in the record books today.

A fiberglass pole allows the athlete to use momentum to catapult higher distances.

Costly Celebration

John Velses had one world record momentarily taken away by spectators. On February 2, 1962, he was the first to vault over 16 feet. However, jubilant fans rushed in and knocked into the crossbars before officials could measure the accurate distance. His vault was disqualified. However, he cleared 16 feet the following day—this time without incident.

Track & Field

Date of Origin
1800s
Place of Origin
Scotland
Legendary Performers
Parry O'Brien, Jr.,
Randy Barnes
Governing Body
International Amateur
Athletic Federation
Where They Compete
Worldwide
Championship Events
World Championships,
Olympic Games

Shot put is a field event in which a heavy ball called the *shot* is pushed, or *put*. This event is a test of strength.

Equipment

The shot is a smooth metallic ball. For men's competition, the shot is approximately 4.75 inches (110 millimeters) in diameter and weighs 16 pounds (7.26 kilograms). Women use a shot that is 4 inches (95 millimeters) in diameter and weighs 8.8 pounds (4 kilograms). Athletes may apply resin to their hands for a better grip.

The *circle* from which the athletes put the shot is 7 feet (2.14 meters) in diameter. It has a raised *stop board* at the front. The shot must land between two *lanes* that protrude from the circle's center at a 40-degree angle.

The Event

The athlete must start in a still position in the circle. Using only one hand, he or she cradles the shot between the shoulder and chin. Rules forbid the athlete from lowering the shot below this starting position, and the athlete cannot throw it from behind the shoulder line. The athlete must remain inside the circle until the shot has landed. The throw is measured from the inside of the circle to the nearest mark made by the shot.

Shot putting originated hundreds of years ago when soldiers competed in tossing cannonballs. In the twelfth century, Londoners enjoyed a contest in which they threw stones of various sizes.

However, the modern form appears to have been part of the first Highland Games in Scotland in the 1800s.

American Jackie Joyner-Kersee about to thrust maximum energy into the put of her shot.

Track & Field

Date of Origin
Approximately 1800
Place of Origin
England
Legendary Performers
**Jozef Schmidt,
Jonathan Edwards**
Governing Body
**International Amateur
Athletic Federation**
Where They Compete
Worldwide
Championship Events
**Olympic Games,
World Championships**

The triple jump is a field event in which athletes dash down a *runway*, then hop, step, and jump into the *landing area*. It is included in all major track and field meets.

Equipment

Runways used in this event are 148 feet (45 meters) long and 4 feet (1.22 meters) wide. The runway has an 8-inch (20-centimeter) wide white wooden board called the *takeoff board*. A *takeoff line* running along the board's end closest to the pit indicates the point beyond which no athlete may step.

An additional 42.8 feet (13 meters) of runway after the takeoff board allows the athletes to perform the hop, step, and jump before they leap into the landing area. The landing area, or pit, is a pit of sand 9 feet 9 inches (3 meters) wide and 29 feet 6 inches (9 meters) long.

The Event

Athletes gain momentum as they run down the track and hit the takeoff board. The athletes then push off on either foot, hit the runway with the same foot (this forms the hop), leap to land on the opposite foot (step), then jump into the pit. Immediately upon landing, they propel forward to avoid falling back and leaving an impression closer to the takeoff board.

Athletes receive either three or six jumps, depending on how many contestants have entered the event. If two or more athletes record the same distance, the winner is the one among them with the next-best jump. Each attempt is measured by officials from the takeoff line to the nearest mark (called a *break*) made in the sand by any body part.

The triple jump requires outstanding body control and explosive leg strength.

Track & Field

Date of Origin
776 B.C.
Place of Origin
Greece
Legendary Performers
Jesse Owens,
Florence Griffith Joyner,
Carl Lewis,
Donovan Bailey
Governing Bodies
International Amateur
Athletic Federation,
Amateur Athletic Union,
U.S.A. Track and Field
Where They Compete
Worldwide
Championship Events
Olympic Games,
World Championships

The 100-meter dash is an event that showcases pure speed. The winner of the event at the international level is proclaimed the world's fastest runner.

Equipment

The 100-meter dash is held on a synthetic, all-weather track. The 100-meter event occurs on a straight section with eight *lanes*, 4 feet (1.22 meters) wide each.

Starting blocks are attached to a *rack*. They can be adjusted for different angles. Athletes wear lightweight shorts and shirts. Most wear special spiked track shoes for better traction.

The Event

Most competitions hold qualifying races to determine which eight runners compete in the finals. Once the field is narrowed to the eight qualifying winners, the final race is held to determine the overall winner.

The competitors gather in their own lanes at the starting line. When the official announces, "On your mark," the runners adopt a semi-kneeling position with both feet on starting blocks. Both hands must be touching the ground. When the announcer says, "Get set," they change to a position in which the body leans forward, the arms and legs are more rigid, and the eyes look straight down. When the official fires the starting pistol, all athletes may begin racing.

If any competitor leaves the starting blocks before the pistol is fired, a *false start* is declared and all runners must return to the starting blocks. If the same runner commits a second false start, he or she is disqualified.

By 100-meter dash standards, this finish would be considered a blowout.

Competitors in this event must remain in their own lanes throughout the race. Pure speed is a gift of all sprinters, but excellent form separates the good from the great. Runners are taught to race with the body in a relaxed state. Tension negatively affects the speed of the runner.

The winner is the individual who first reaches the *finish line* with any part of his or her torso (the portion of the body from the neck to the midsection). A runner may not extend the arms or head in an attempt to touch the finish line first.

In 1935, Jesse Owens tied the world record for 100 meters at Ohio State. That same day, he set or equaled six world records.

History

The first Greek Olympic Games, held in 776 B.C., included a footrace. Over the next eleven centuries, the Greeks met every four years to conduct this and other events. The Olympics continued until the Roman emperor Theodosius banned them in A.D. 394. As a result, track and field meets disappeared from Europe for much of the Middle Ages.

In 1895, the New York Athletic Club competed against the London Athletic Club in the first international meet. The next year Athens, Greece, hosted the first modern Olympic Games.

One of the most famous athletes to perform in the 100-meter dash was Jesse Owens. He captured the gold medal in this event and three others in the 1936 Olympic Games. In more recent times, American athletes Carl Lewis and Florence Griffith Joyner enjoyed immense success in the event. Canada's Donovan Bailey set a world record time of 9.84 seconds during the 1996 Olympic Games.

A Fighter Since Birth

Wilma Rudolph battled a succession of childhood illnesses to become a world-class sprinter. Weighing less than five pounds at birth, Rudolph was stricken with pneumonia and scarlet fever that left her handicapped. Through determination—and good luck—she gradually regained use of her legs. She went on to win three gold medals at the 1960 Olympics.

Track & Field

The 200-meter dash features sprinting around a curved section of the track as well as a straightaway.

Equipment

The 200-meter dash is held on a synthetic, all-weather oval track. The race starts on a curved portion of the track, then finishes on a straight section with eight *lanes*, 4 feet (1.22 meters) wide each.

Starting blocks are attached to a *rack*. The blocks can be adjusted to different angles, but the starting blocks may not have springs or any other item that provides assistance.

The Event

Depending on the number of entrants, most competitions hold qualifying races to determine which eight runners compete in the finals. Once the field is narrowed to the eight qualifying winners, the final race is held to determine the overall winner.

The competitors gather in their own lanes at the starting line. When the official announces, "On your mark," the runners adopt a semi-kneeling position with both feet on starting blocks, which helps give the athletes a stronger start. Both hands must be touching the ground. When the announcer says, "Get set," they change to a position in which the body leans forward, the arms and legs are more rigid, and the eyes look straight down. When the official fires the starting pistol, all athletes may begin racing.

A runner can be disqualified if he or she leaves the starting block too soon. If the individual takes off before the pistol is fired, it's declared a false start and all the runners must return to the starting position. If this happens twice, the guilty runner is disqualified.

Marion Jones holds the world record in the 200-meter dash with a time of 21.8 seconds.

Once the runners leave the starting blocks, they must remain in their own lanes until the race is complete. The winner is the individual who first reaches the *finish line* with any part of his or her torso (the portion of the body from the neck to the midsection). A runner may not extend the arms or head in an attempt to touch the finish line first.

Races are usually timed by electronic photo-timers that measure to .01 of a second. If a tie is declared, it stands as the final result unless the race is a qualifying race. In that case, the tying athletes run again.

The top runners of the world vie for the gold medal in the 200-meter dash at the 1999 World Track and Field Championships.

History

Like all other races, the 200-meter dash has its origins in the ancient Greek Olympic Games. The first Greek Olympic Games, held in 776 B.C., included a footrace, and over the next eleven centuries the Greeks met every four years to conduct this and other events. These spectacles were revered by the ancient Greeks because of the great emphasis they placed on physical fitness.

Back on Track

After an absence of nearly 1,000 years, track and field events staged a comeback in the 1100s, when English athletes used fields and roads for races. So many young men took up the activities that a series of English kings tried to ban the sport. However, repeated opposition forced the government to back down, and by the 1500s track and field was an accepted activity.

One of the most famous athletes to perform in the 200-meter dash was Jesse Owens, who captured the gold medal in this event and three others in the 1936 Olympic Games. Wilma Rudolph starred in women's racing in the 1960s, while Florence Griffith Joyner enjoyed immense success in the event. Michael Johnson of the United States set a world record time of 19.32 seconds in 1996.

Track & Field

The 400-meter dash is one lap around an outdoor track and two around an indoor track. Runners race at nearly full speed through the entire event. It usually ends in a furious rush that sees two or three runners just hundredths of seconds apart.

Equipment

The 400-meter dash is held on a synthetic, all-weather oval track with eight *lanes*, 4 feet (1.22 meters) wide each. It begins on a curved portion of the track, then finishes on a straight section.

Athletes wear lightweight shorts and shirts. Most wear special spiked track shoes for better traction.

The Event

Depending upon the number of entrants, most competitions hold qualifying races called *heats* to determine which eight runners compete in the finals. The number of heats depends on how many athletes enter the competition, and the heats are usually arranged so that the best runners do not face each other until the final event. Once the field is narrowed to the eight qualifying winners, the final race is held to determine the overall winner.

The competitors gather in their own lanes at the *starting line*. Since they must remain in their lanes at all times (and since the runners in the outside lanes must cover more distance to make one complete circuit of the track), the starting line is staggered. The runner in the outside lane starts slightly ahead of

U.S. track star Michael Johnson runs one lap around the track in under 44 seconds.

Cuba's Alberto Juantorena gained fame with two Olympic gold medals, in the 400-meter and 800-meter races in 1976. A woman from the United States accomplished something similar in 1984, at the Los Angeles Olympics. Valerie Brisco-Hooks became the first female athlete to win the 200-meter dash and the 400-meter dash in the same Olympics.

the runner in the lane next to him or her. The runner on the inside lane starts farthest back. In this manner, they all race 400 meters to the same *finish line*.

The winner is the individual who first reaches the finish line with any part of his or her torso (the portion of the body from the neck to the midsection). Speed is a major factor in the 400-meter dash, but length of stride is also important.

History

Like all other races, the 400-meter dash has its origins in the ancient Greek Olympic Games. The first Greek Olympic Games, held in 776 B.C., included a footrace, and over the next eleven centuries the Greeks met every four years to conduct this and other events.

Centuries later, in 1912, sixteen nations formed the International Amateur Athletic Federation. The organization recognizes world records in over seventy men's and women's events and is the sport's governing body.

In the 1960 Olympic Games Otis Davis completed a double victory by capturing the gold medal in both the 1,600-meter (4 x 400-meter) relay and the 400-meter dash. In more recent times Butch Reynolds of the United States and Marita Koch of Germany set records in the event. Reynolds ran a record time of 43.29 seconds in 1988, a record that was still standing more than a decade later. Koch ran a time of 47.60 seconds in 1985. Her record, too, was still standing fifteen years later. Michael Johnson set the Olympic record in the 400-meter dash in Atlanta with a time of 43.49 seconds. Johnson also holds the world indoor record. His time of 44.63 set in 1995 has not been bested.

Valerie Brisco-Hooks holds the American women's record, running it in 48.83 seconds in 1984.

Track & Field

Date of Origin
1864
Place of Origin
England
Legendary Performers
Willie Davenport,
Colin Jackson
Governing Bodies
International Amateur
Athletic Federation,
U.S.A. Track and Field
Where They Compete
Worldwide
Championship Events
Olympic Games,
World Championships

Hurdle events are short races in which the competitor must jump over a series of ten fence-like obstacles called *hurdles*. This event requires speed, timing, and dexterity.

Equipment

The 110-meter hurdles is held on a synthetic, all-weather track. While the track is oval in shape, the race occurs on a straight section with eight *lanes*, 4 feet (1.2 meters) wide each.

The hurdles are L-shaped metal frames 4 feet (1.2 meters) wide and 3.5 feet (1.1 meters) high connected with a wooden top bar. They are balanced so that they topple forward if an athlete lightly taps them with the foot as he or she vaults over. The first hurdle stands 45.6 feet (13.72 meters) from the *starting line*, and the final hurdle stands 46.6 feet (14.02 meters) from the *finish line*. The ten hurdles are 30.5 feet (9.14 meters) apart.

Athletes wear lightweight shorts and shirts. Most wear special spiked track shoes for better traction.

The Event

Depending on the number of entrants, most competitions hold qualifying races to determine which eight runners compete in the finals. Once the field is narrowed to the eight qualifying winners, the final race is held to determine the overall winner.

The competitors gather in their own lanes at the *starting line*. When the official fires the starting pistol, all athletes may begin racing.

Once the runners leave the *starting blocks*, they must remain in their own lanes until the race is

The 110-meter hurdles at the seventh World Track and Field Championships held in Seville, Spain.

Athletes kick their lead leg directly forward and swing their rear leg over to clear the hurdle.

complete. A hurdler is disqualified if he or she trails a foot alongside the hurdle during a leap, purposely knocks over a hurdle with the hand, or jumps any hurdle not in his or her lane.

The runner may take off from either foot in clearing a hurdle. The other leg is lifted straight across the top bar in a direct line with the line of running. The athlete leans forward as the back leg is lifted over the hurdle for a smooth landing.

History

Hurdling started in 1850 as part of a steeplechase event, a long run filled with various obstacles. The first race strictly using hurdles occurred in 1864 at Oxford University in England. The runners jumped over sheep hurdles—portable fencing made from interwoven branches and designed to control the movement of sheep. The height of those early sheep hurdles was 3.6 feet, about the same height used today in the 110-meter hurdles.

At first authorities disqualified a runner if he or she knocked over three or more hurdles. The International Amateur Athletic Federation removed the rule in 1932 so that runners could focus more attention on speed. Runners still try to clear every hurdle. Each time they jar an obstacle, they are slightly slowed.

In 1993, Colin Jackson of Great Britain broke the world record in the 110-meter hurdles with a time of 12.91 seconds. The women's event is ten meters less. Yordenkia Donkova of Bulgaria holds the 100-meter hurdles world record with a time of 12.21 seconds.

Career Olympian

American runner Willie Davenport was one of the greatest athletes to compete in the 110-meter hurdles. He participated in five different Olympics between 1964 and 1980, winning a gold medal in the event in 1968 and a bronze medal in 1976. Davenport showed his versatility by participating in the 1980 Winter Olympics as a member of the U.S. bobsled team.

Track & Field

Hurdle events are short races in which the competitor must jump over a series of ten fencelike obstacles called *hurdles*. The race encompasses one lap around the track.

Equipment

The 400-meter hurdles is held on a synthetic, all-weather track. The hurdles are spread equally along the entire track. Each of the eight lanes is 4 feet (1.22 meters) wide.

The hurdles are L-shaped metal frames that are 4 feet (1.2 meters) wide and 3 feet (1.7 meters) high for men and 2.5 feet (.8 meters) high for women. The metal frames are connected with a wooden top bar. The first hurdle stands 150 feet (45 meters) from the starting line, and the final hurdle stands 133 feet (40 meters) from the finish line. The ten hurdles are 117 feet (35 meters) apart.

The Event

When clearing the hurdle, the upper body leans forward to maintain strong momentum.

The 400-meter hurdles is held for both male and female athletes. Once the runners leave the *starting blocks*, they must remain in their own lanes until the race is complete. A hurdler is disqualified if he or she trails a foot alongside the hurdle during a leap, purposely knocks over a hurdle with the hand, or jumps any hurdle not in his or her lane. Runners lean forward as they leap to maintain speed and momentum.

Before 1932, runners were disqualified if they knocked over three or more hurdles, but the International Athletic Federation changed the rule so athletes could focus on running faster. Today, if a runner clips or knocks over a hurdle, it may adversely affect his or her time and

Pure Dominance

No one dominated the 400 meter hurdles like American runner, Edwin Moses. In the 1976 Olympics, Moses won the gold medal in a world-record time of 47.64 seconds. He lowered his own record three more times during his career, reaching 47.02 seconds in 1983. In 1977, Moses won the World Cup 400-meter hurdles in Dusseldorf, West Germany, beginning a string of 122 consecutive victories. He added a second gold medal in 1984 and a bronze medal in 1988. Moses is enshrined in the Olympic Hall of Fame.

possibly his or her landing, but they are not penalized.

The 400-meter race can be much more difficult than the 110-meter hurdle race. Not only is the race longer, but five of the hurdles rest on a curved portion of the track. This makes it very difficult to maintain balance, speed, and position in the correct lane.

History

The 400-meter hurdles race originated in England in 1864. The United States has dominated the men's 400-meter hurdles event since its Olympic birth in 1900. There have been 21 400-meter hurdle event gold-medals distributed and 16 belong to American athletes. The U.S. won six straight gold medals in the event from 1936 to 1964. Glenn Davis won back-to-back golds in 1956 and 1960.

Track legend Edwin Moses won the gold in 1976, but was unable to attempt a repeat due to the Americans boycotting the 1980 Olympics in Moscow. He returned to win the gold in 1984. Moses, who studied physics at Morehouse College on an academic scholarship, started hurdling as a hobby. He honed an unstoppable, thirteen-step pace between hurdles.

The women's 400-meter hurdles race did not become an Olympic event until 1984. Nawal el Moutawakel or Morocco earned the first gold medal with a time of 54.61 seconds. Deon Hemmings of Jamaica won the gold medal in 1996 finishing in an Olympic record time 52.82 seconds.

American Kevin Young set the world record during the 1992 Olympics in Barcelona with a time of 46.78 seconds. Kim Batten recorded the fastest time ever in 1995 in Sweden, finishing in 52.61 seconds.

Track & Field

The 800-meter race is an intense endurance race. Runners build speed as the race progresses and ends in a sprint.

Date of Origin
776 B.C.
Place of Origin
Greece
Legendary Performers
Peter Snell,
Sebastian Coe
Governing Bodies
International Amateur
Athletic Federation,
U.S.A. Track and Field
Where They Compete
Worldwide
Championship Events
Olympic Games,
World Championships

Equipment

The 800-meter event is held on a synthetic, all-weather oval track with eight *lanes*, 4 feet (1.22 meters) wide each. The 800-meter race starts on a curved portion of the track, then finishes on a straight section.

Athletes wear lightweight shorts and shirts. For better traction, most wear special spiked track shoes with up to eleven spikes on the sole. However, track shoes are not mandatory. Some runners compete barefoot.

The Event

Most competitions hold qualifying races called *heats* to determine which eight runners compete in the finals. The number of heats depends on how many athletes enter the competition. Heats are arranged so the best runners do not face each other until the final event.

The competitors gather in their own lanes at the *starting line*. While the starting line is staggered, as in the 400-meter dash, the runners are allowed to leave their lanes. They must wait until they've rounded the first curve on the track and reach the straightaway before leaving their lanes. From that moment on, runners may vie for the inside position as long as they do not run into or block another runner. The race consists of two complete circuits on

An athlete must possess speed and endurance to achieve success in the 800-meter race.

the typical outdoor track and four circuits on an indoor track.

When the official fires the starting pistol, all athletes may begin racing. If any competitor leaves before the pistol is fired, a *false start* is declared and all runners must return to the *starting blocks*. If the same runner commits a second false start, he or she is disqualified.

History

Like many other races, the 800-meter event has its origins in the ancient Greek Olympic Games. The first Greek Olympic Games, held in 776 B.C., included a footrace, and over the next eleven centuries the Greeks met every four years to conduct this and other events.

Records of an 1154 English track meet exist, and the English participated in Robert Dover's "Olympick Games" in the 1600s and the Much Wenlock Games in the 1800s. England formed the first track and field club, the Necton Guild, in 1817, and conducted its first national championship in 1866. Track meets were open only to male athletes until early in the 1900s, when the Olympic Games began including women's track events.

In 1976, a Cuban sprinter, Alberto Juantorena, became the first male athlete to win both the 400-meter and 800-meter races in a single Olympics. In 1981 Britain's Sebastian Coe ran the 800-meter race in 1 minute 41.73 seconds, while Jarmila Kratochvilova of Czechoslovakia clocked a 1 minute 53.28 seconds race in 1983.

Wilson Kipketer of Denmark dominated the men's 800-meter race from 1995. He won three consecutive World Track and Field championship titles in 1995, 1997, and 1999. Kipketer also set the world record in 1997 during a track meet in Cologne, Germany, with a time of 1 minute 41.11 seconds. Despite his excellence, Kipketer has never won an Olympic gold medal.

Track & Field

The 1,500-meter race combines speed and endurance. The distance is just short of one mile.

Date of Origin
776 B.C.
Place of Origin
Greece
Legendary Performers
Paavo Nurmi,
Sebastian Coe
Governing Bodies
International Amateur
Athletic Federation,
U.S.A. Track and Field
Where They Compete
Worldwide
Championship Events
Olympic Games,
World Championships

Equipment

The 1,500-meter event is held on a synthetic, all-weather oval track. The race starts on a straight section of the track, and completes 3.75 circuits of an outdoor track and 7.5 circuits of an indoor track.

The Event

The competitors gather along the *starting line*, but once the race begins no *lanes* are used. From that moment on, runners may vie for the inside position as long as they do not run into or block another runner.

Runners usually devise a plan heading into the race. Some try to take a quick lead and sustain it throughout the race. Others conserve their energy for an all-out sprint toward the end. Both methods have proven successful.

When run by world-class athletes, the 1,500-meter race can seem like a sprint.

Modern training equipment and techniques have radically enhanced performance and improved running times for this event. Runners are faster and possess greater endurance. Comparing today's times with times from the past illustrates this point. In 1896, Edwin Flack of Australia won the gold medal by running 1,500 meters in 4 minutes 33.2 seconds. One hundred years later, Noureddine Morceli of Algeria claimed the gold medal in the same event. His winning time was 3 minutes 35.78 seconds; nearly a minute better than Flack's time.

Mr. Sandman

If you think running an endurance race is difficult, try sprinting up and down sand dunes. That is one way that Australia's Herb Elliott trained, and the technique certainly reaped dividends. The brilliant athlete won 44 straight races in the 1,500 meter race and the mile event in the late 1950s and early 1960s.

History

American runner Jim Lightbody was the first to win the 1,500-meter race in consecutive Olympics. In 1904, he recorded a winning time of 4 minutes 5.4 seconds. Lightbody returned to the 1906 Olympic Games to earn his second gold medal despite finishing with a time nearly seven seconds slower (4 minutes 12 seconds).

Pavo Nurmi of Finland gained fame in the 1920s in this event. He won the gold medal in the 1924 Olympics, drawing attention and prestige to the 1,500-meter event. Nurmi was one of the greatest distance runners of all time. He added gold medals in the 5,000- and 10,000-meter races between 1920 and 1928.

England's Sebastian Coe set eleven world records during his illustrious career, including one in the 1,500-meter race. He won the gold medal in the 1980 and 1984 Olympics, becoming the first 1,500-meter runner to win two consecutive Olympics since Lightbody did it in 1904 and 1906.

Noureddine Morceli dominated the event in the 1990s, winning three track and field world championships, and an Olympic gold medal in 1996. Hichan El Guerrouj of Morocco holds the men's record with a time of 3 minutes 26 seconds. China's Qu Yunxia established the women's record with a time of 3 minutes 50.46 seconds.

One of the most exciting 1,500-meter races took place in the 1992 Olympic Games held in Barcelona, Spain. Fermin Cacho of Spain ran the race of a lifetime, claiming the gold medal in front of a frenzied home crowd. Cacho was the only Spaniard (man or woman) to win a gold medal in the track and field events in Barcelona.

Track & Field

The 5,000-meter race is an endurance race in which athletes try to be the first to cross the *finish line*. The race is just over three miles in distance. World-class runners run this race at a pace of just over four minutes per mile.

Equipment

The 5,000-meter event is held on a synthetic, all-weather oval track. The race starts on a straight section of the track, and completes 12.5 circuits of an outdoor track and 25 circuits of an indoor track.

Athletes wear lightweight shorts and shirts. Most wear special spiked track shoes for better traction.

The Event

The athletes gather along the *starting line*, but once the race begins no *lanes* are used. From that moment on, runners may vie for the inside position as long as they do not run into or block another runner. Competitors run in a counterclockwise direction around the track.

The 5,000-meter race is approximately 12.5 laps around the track.

The winner is the individual who first reaches the finish line with any part of his or her torso (the portion of the body from the neck to the midsection). A runner may not extend the arms or head in an attempt the touch the finish line first.

Paavo Nurmi of Finland and Czechoslovakia's acclaimed Emil Zátopek gained fame in this event in the 1920s and 1950s. The men's record was set in 1998 by Ethiopia's Haile Gebrselassie with a time of 12 minutes 39.36 seconds. In 1999 Jiang Bo of China set a new women's world record in the 5,000-meter race with a time of 14 minutes, 29.09 seconds. She surpassed the record set by Fernanda Ribiero by 8 seconds.

Track & Field

The 10,000-meter race is a race for well-conditioned athletes. It is approximately 6.25 miles.

Equipment

The 10,000-meter event is held on a synthetic, all-weather oval track. The 10,000-meter race starts on a straight section of the track, and completes 25 circuits of an outdoor track and 50 circuits of an indoor track.

The Event

Most meets hold qualifying races called *heats* to determine which eight runners compete in the finals. The number of heats depends on how many athletes enter the competition, and the heats are arranged so that the best runners do not face each other until the final event.

The competitors gather along the *starting line*, but once the race begins no *lanes* are used. From that moment on, runners may vie for the inside position as long as they do not run into or block another runner. Competitors run in a counterclockwise direction around the track.

The 10,000-meter race was not an Olympic event for women until 1988. Olga Bondarenko of the Soviet Union earned the distinction of becoming the first woman to win Olympic gold in the event. China's Wang Junxia holds the women's world record for the 10,000-meter race with a time of 29 minutes 31.78 seconds. Haile Gebrselassie of Ethiopia set the men's world record in 1998 with a time of 26 minutes 22.75 seconds.

Mental toughness is sometimes the only factor separating first place from fifth place.

Track & Field

Date of Origin
776 B.C.
Place of Origin
Greece
Legendary Performers
Jesse Owens,
Wilma Rudolph,
Carl Lewis
Governing Bodies
International Amateur
Athletic Federation,
U.S.A. Track and Field
Where They Compete
Worldwide
Championship Events
Olympic Games,
World Championships

This race is one of two relay races in which four runners team together to complete the race. The relay team must complete one lap around the track. The athletes take turns running an equal portion of the race.

Equipment

The 4 × 100-meter event is held on a synthetic, all-weather track. The oval track has eight *lanes*, 4 feet (1.22 meters) wide each. A *takeover zone* is marked on the track and designates the area in which each runner must hand over the *baton* to the next runner.

The baton is a hollow tube about 1 foot (30 centimeters) long. Each runner must carry it in his or her hand at all times and pass it to the next runner on the team.

The Event

Squads determine the order in which the four members run their 100 meters. The first athlete for each team steps to the *starting blocks* with the baton in his or her hand and adopts a semi-kneeling position, which helps give the athlete a stronger start. Both hands must be touching the ground. When the announcer says, "Get set," the athletes change to a position in which the body leans forward, the arms and legs are more rigid. When the official fires the starting pistol, all athletes may begin racing.

Once the runners leave the starting blocks, they must remain in their own lanes. They race 100 meters (100.9 yards) to the takeover zone, a 20-meter-long (21.8 yards) section of track where they pass the baton to the next runner. The receiver cannot begin running more than 10 meters (10.9 yards) behind the takeover zone. If

The slightest mistake passing the baton can change the outcome of a 4 × 100 meter race.

the baton is passed outside the takeover zone, the team is disqualified. If the baton is dropped, the runner who dropped it must pick it up and resume running.

The Takeover Zone

One of the trickiest parts of a relay race is handing the baton to the next runner. The two athletes must properly time their running to avoid losing precious split seconds, and they must be certain to hand off the baton within the 20-meter zone, which is marked with white lines. To save time, the front runner tries not to look back toward the teammate.

The procedure is followed in similar fashion for the second and third runners. The fourth runner, called the *anchor*, completes the final 100 meters.

History

The 4 x 100-meter relay has its origins in ancient times. Greek athletes engaged in a series of athletic contests, culminating in the first Olympic Games in 776 B.C. Track and field events were introduced in England in the 1100s, but were not popular until the 1800s, when different schools conducted interclass meets.

In 1936 Jesse Owens was on the team that won a gold medal in this race, one of the four gold medals he won in the Olympics that year. American runner Wilma Rudolph helped the United States win this event in the 1960 Olympic Games. It was one of her three gold medals.

Athletes benefit from improved training methods, and synthetic tracks provide more spring than earlier tracks. Financial assistance from different groups, such as the United States Olympic Committee, gives athletes more time to focus on practice.

Numerous track and field records have fallen in recent years, including the record for the 4 x 100-meters. The team of Carl Lewis, Mike Marsh, Leroy Burrell, and Dennis Mitchell ran a world record time of 37.4 seconds at the 1992 Olympics in Barcelona. That time was equaled in 1993 at the World Track and Field Championships in Stuttgart, Germany. A U.S. team of Jon Drummond, Andre Cason, Dennis Mitchell, and Leroy Burrell tied the world record.

Track & Field

This is one of two relay races in which four runners team together to complete the race. In the 4 × 400-meter relay, each athlete runs one lap around the track.

Equipment

The 4 × 400-meter event is held on a synthetic, all-weather track containing eight *lanes*, 4 feet (1.22 meters) wide. A *takeover zone* is marked on the track and designates the area in which each runner must hand over the *baton* to the next runner.

The baton is a hollow tube about 1 foot (30 centimeters) long. Each runner must carry it in his or her hand at all times and pass it to the next runner on the team.

The Event

Michael Johnson receives the baton from teammate Angelo Taylor to run the final leg of the 4 × 400-meter relay at the World Track and Field Championships in Seville, Spain.

Squads determine the order in which the four members run their 400 meters. The first athlete for each team steps to the *starting blocks* with the baton in his or her hand and adopts a semi-kneeling position, which helps give the athlete a stronger start.

Once the runners leave the starting blocks, they must remain in their own lanes until after the second runner completes the first turn. They may then attempt to move to the inside lane. They race 400 meters (437.4 yards) to the takeover zone, a 20-meter-long (21.8 yards) section of track where they pass the baton to the next runner, who cannot begin running more than 10 meters (10.9 yards) behind the takeover zone. If the baton is handed over outside the takeover zone, the team is disqualified. Runners must be in their own lanes for the takeover unless they can complete the maneuver without interfering with another team. After handing over the baton, the first runner should remain in the lane until all other teams have passed through the takeover zone.

The procedure is followed in similar fashion for the second and third runners. The fourth runner, called the *anchor*, completes the final 400 meters, and the winner is the team whose final runner first touches the finish line with any part of his or her torso.

History

The 4 x 400-meter relay has its origins in ancient times. Greek athletes engaged in a series of athletic contests, culminating in the first Olympic Games in 776 B.C.

One of the most talented runners in the 4 x 400-meter relay was Glenn Davis. In 1960 he successfully defended his 1956 gold medal performance in the 400-meter hurdles, then teamed with three other Americans to capture the gold in the 4 x 400-meter relay race. Davis was enshrined in the U.S. Olympic Hall of Fame for his efforts. The world record is held by Americans Michael Johnson, Jerome Young, Antonio Pettigrew, and Tyree Washington. They set the record in 1998 with a time of 2 minutes 54.2 seconds.

Since 1972, only three countries have claimed the gold medal in the women's 4 x 400-meter relay race. The East Germans won the gold in 1972 and 1976. The USSR (now Russia, Ukraine, Belarus, and other countries) won the gold in 1980, set a world record in 1988, and won as the Unified Team in 1992. The United States earned gold medals in 1984 and 1996. The world record set in 1988 still stands today. Tatyana Ledovskaya, Olga Nazarova, Maria Pinigina, and Olga Bryzgina of the USSR set the mark in 3 minutes 15.17 seconds.

Trampolining

Trampolining is a sport in which a person bounces from a *trampoline* to perform acrobatic feats in the air.

Date of Origin	**1936**
Place of Origin	**United States**
Legendary Performer	**George Nissen**
Governing Body	**International Trampoline Association**
Where They Compete	**Worldwide**
Championship Events	**World Championships, Nissen Cup**

Equipment

Trampolines are either circular or rectangular in shape. The surface upon which the athlete bounces is made from solid or woven material. It is attached to a frame by rubber cords or steel springs. The standard trampoline is 17 feet (5.1 meters) long and 9.5 feet (2.9 meters) wide. Thick pads, called *safety platforms*, are attached to the two short ends as protection for the athlete.

The Event

In American amateur competition, performers must execute six basic stunts while bouncing into the air—a *feet bounce, hands and knees drop, knees drop, seat drop, front drop,* and *back drop.* The athlete may also insert somersaults and twists as he or she completes each stunt. Judges award points based on proper form and balance. The two main governing bodies in the United States are the Amateur Athletic Union and the National Collegiate Athletic Association.

The first trampoline made specifically for jumping appeared in the United States in 1936. George Nissen, a diving and tumbling champion, created the apparatus.

Another form of the sport is synchronized trampolining. Two trampolines are used side by side and two performers of the same team carry out identical routines. They attempt to keep in time with each other as closely as possible.

Young kids flip over the sport of trampolining.

Trotting

Trotting is a form of horse racing in which each horse pulls a lightweight, two-wheeled cart called a *sulky* or *racing bike*.

Date of Origin
1890s
Place of Origin
United States
Legendary Performers
Delvin Miller, Bill Houghton, John Campbell
Governing Bodies
U.S. Trotting Association, Standardbred Canada
Where They Compete
North America, Scandinavia, Holland, Germany
Championship Events
Hambletonian, Kentuck Futurity, Yonkers Trot

Equipment

Horses used in trotting are called *standardbreds*. They are bred from *thoroughbred* horses and sturdy farm or work horses. The thorough-breds are known for their speed. Farm horses are known for their rugged strength and gait (running style).

A sulky consists of a lightweight wooden or duralumin (soft steel) frame mounted on ball-bearing bicycle wheels. It seats one *driver* who controls the direction and pace of the horse.

The Event

The rhythmic, characteristic movement of a horse's feet and legs in motion is called a gait. Standardbred horses are divided into two groups characterized by their gait: *trotters* and *pacers*. In competition, the horse must perform this gait throughout the entire race.

The trot is a more natural gait. It's a rapid, two-beat diagonal gait. The forefoot on one side and the opposite hind foot take off and strike the ground at the same time. It's essential that the trotter is balanced evenly on both diagonals. The weight of the horse is distributed first by one diagonal and then the opposite diagonal. Then all four feet are off the ground at the same time for an instant. The other form of gait, pacing, moves the front and hind feet on the same side forward and back together at the same time.

Drivers control and instruct their horse from the sulky.

Most trotting races are one mile in distance. The smallest racetrack is 0.5-miles. The longest is 1.25 miles.

Volleyball

Volleyball is an indoor or outdoor team sport in which players hit a ball back and forth across a *net* with their arms or hands. The game is popular worldwide.

Equipment

A *volleyball court* measures 59 feet (18 meters) long and 29.5 feet (9 meters) wide. A mesh net 8 feet (2.4 meters) high for men and 7.4 feet (2.2 meters) for women divides the court into two equal 30-foot (9-meter) squares. The *service areas* are behind the back *boundary lines* at the right ends. An indoor court is made of wood or synthetic material, while outdoor courts are marked off on grass or sand.

The leathery ball measures 25 to 27 inches (64 to 69 centimeters) around and weighs 9.5 ounces (270 grams). Players wear shorts, shirts, and soft-soled shoes.

The Event

Indoor volleyball features two teams of six players, but outdoor volleyball can field two, three, four, or six players on a team.

The game begins with one player standing in the service area and hitting the ball across the net into the opponent's side. The other team must return the ball before it bounces on the floor, and play continues until either one side fails to return the ball or the ball flies out of bounds. No player may strike the ball twice in succession, nor may anyone catch the ball. The receiving team cannot hit the ball more than three times before it crosses the net, nor may they *carry* a pass to a teammate.

Rafa Pascual of Spain spikes the ball over the net during a World League volleyball competition.

170

If the receiving team fails to return the ball, the serving team earns one *point*. If the serving team is unsuccessful, service switches to the other team. At each change of service, the players rotate position clockwise. The first team to reach fifteen points with a two-point lead wins the game. If the score is tied at fourteen, the game is extended. A regular game is extended until one team gains a two-point lead or scores the seventeenth point. A deciding game is extended until a two-point lead is reached.

History

In 1895 William G. Morgan, a Young Men's Christian Association (YMCA) physical education instructor in Holyoke, Massachusetts, started volleyball. He hoped to create a sport for senior citizens that was not as demanding as basketball. Morgan called his game "mintonette."

Five years later the YMCA developed a set of rules for the sport, and in 1916 the National Collegiate Athletic Association adopted those rules. The United States Volleyball Association began supervising the sport in 1928.

Today, at least 250 million people play competitive volleyball worldwide, and over eight hundred million play for recreation. The game's simplicity and its availability make it extremely popular. Volleyball is governed worldwide by the International Volleyball Federation, which started in 1947.

Jackie Silva of Brazil hits a bump shot during the 1997 Beach Volleyball World Championship.

Spiking

One of the most aggressive forms of hitting a volleyball is called *spiking*. In this, a player tries to spike, or *slam*, the ball past opposing players so that it smacks onto the floor before the receivers can touch it or bounces off a player's body before he or she can prepare for the ball. Both spectators and players enjoy this exciting aspect of the game.

Walking Events

Walking events, also called race walking, are one of the most unique forms of athletic competition. Walking events are very popular in Europe.

Equipment

Walking events take place either on an existing road or on a track. Competitors wear lightweight shorts and shirts, plus special track shoes. The shoes used for race walking are more robust and heavier than those used in track competition.

The Event

The entrants must race according to a rigid form. Since each athlete must maintain continuous contact with the ground, one foot must touch the ground before the other foot is lifted. While the foot is in contact with the ground, the leg must be in a straight position. These requirements, combined with the fact that the athlete achieves the quickest motion by moving the hips from side to side, produce a wobbly motion. If an athlete does not advance in the proper manner, he or she receives either a warning or disqualification.

Standard distances for walking events are the 20-kilometer (12.4-mile) road walk and the 50-kilometer (31.1-mile) road walk. The International Amateur Athletic Federation keeps records in those two events as well as for the 20-mile (32.2-kilometer), 30-mile (48.3-kilometer), and 30-kilometer (18.6-mile) races, and the two-hour race.

Walking events started in the 1700s in England, where spectators bet money on the outcome of races from one city to another. One of the most popular events was the six-day race between London and York. The sport joined the Olympic Games in 1908.

In walking events, the athlete must maintain continuous contact with the ground.

Water Polo

Water polo is a sport between two teams who try to score points by tossing a ball into the opponent's *goal*.

Equipment

The game takes place in a *swimming pool* measuring between 66 and 98 feet (20 to 30 meters) long and 33 to 66 feet (20 to 30 meters) wide. The water must be at least 5.9 feet (1.8 meters) deep. A netted goal at each end is 10 feet (3 meters) wide and 3 feet (0.9 meters) high.

The circular ball weighs between 15 and 16 ounces (400 to 450 grams) and has a circumference of 27 to 28 inches (68 to 71 centimeters).

One team must wear dark blue caps and the other white. Both *goalkeepers* wear red caps. Most caps contain ear protectors. Players wear swimming suits and trunks.

The Event

Each team uses seven players—a goalkeeper, three *defenders*, and three *forwards*. While the goalkeeper is permitted to grasp the ball with both hands, the others may only push or throw the ball with one hand. The object is to outscore the opponent by propelling the ball into the net. Each score is worth one *point*, but counts only if two or more players have touched the ball after the start or restart.

A game lasts four *periods* of seven minutes each, with a two-minute break between periods. In the event of a tie at the end of regulation, teams play two three-minute periods. If necessary, additional sets of three-minute periods are added until one teams wins.

Italy's Ferdinando Gandolfi takes the game-winning shot in a 9-8 overtime victory. The win gave Italy the Olympic gold medal in Barcelona in 1992.

173

Water Skiing

Water skiing is a sport in which an athlete rides across the surface of the water on *skis* while being pulled by a powerboat.

Date of Origin
1925
Place of Origin
United States
Legendary Performers
Bruce Parker,
Billy Spencer
Governing Bodies
American Water Ski
Association,
World Water Ski Union
Where They Compete
Worldwide
Championship Events
United States National
Tournament,
World Water Ski Union,
World Championships

Equipment

Water skiing requires a *powerboat*, a *towline*, a *life jacket*, and skis. The participant leans back in the water, clutches the towline, and waits for the powerboat to lift him or her to the water's surface.

Skis come in various shapes. The *general purpose ski* is about 6 feet (1.8 meters) long, made from wood, with a smooth finish. *Bindings* made of rubber or plastic secure the feet to the ski. Any engine-propelled boat capable of going 20 miles (32 kilometers) per hour can be used for water skiing.

The Events

Water skiing features several competitions. The *slalom* requires the *water skier* to navigate his or her way through anchored buoys on a set course. The typical slalom course runs 283 yards (259 meters) long and 75 feet (23 meters) wide with buoys standing at different intervals. Each athlete receives two runs through the course, and judges award points based upon performance and elapsed time.

Trick skiing demands that the competitors perform as many tricks as possible within twenty seconds. The skier must show that he or she can execute tricks on flat water and on the boat's wake, ski from side to side, ski backwards, step over the towline, and perform twists and turns.

Some water skiing events are performed on a single board rather than a pair of skis.

Where to Begin

Water skiing offers three different methods of starting. In the *deep-water start*, the skier begins in the water and is pulled to the surface by the boat. In the *dock start*, the skier sits on the dock and is pulled into the water. The *scooter start* takes the skier directly from the beach onto the water's surface.

In *ski jumping*, the skier is towed by a boat to a *ramp* coated with wax. The skier vaults from the ramp while still clutching the towline, remains aloft as long as possible to attain greater distance, then settles onto the water's surface. Each athlete receives three attempts, and the best jump counts for the competition.

Ski kite flying has also grown in popularity. Attached to a large kite by a body harness, the skier is towed out into the wind, where the skier will be elevated to heights of up to 100 feet (30.5 meters). While airborne, the skier executes a series of maneuvers or flies a slalom course similar to that on the water.

History

Water skiing is an offshoot of snow skiing, especially ski-tow races. In these events, competitors held onto ropes attached to ponies, which pulled them along the snow.

Ralph Samuelson may have invented water skiing in 1922 by attaching barrel staves to his feet and skiing across a Minnesota lake. However, inventor Fred Waller is generally given credit for creating the sport. Before his skis, many people had glided across lakes on single pieces of flat boards, but Waller used two narrow slats, and in 1925 he received a patent for water skis.

A few years later the sport developed in European resorts along the Mediterranean Sea. When cheaper, faster outboard boats became available in the 1940s, more people turned to water skiing for relaxation, fun, and competition.

The first American contest occurred in 1939 at Jones Beach on New York's Long Island. Bruce Parker, who went on to become a legendary ski performer, captured the inaugural tournament.

Weightlifting

Weightlifting is a sport in which an athlete lifts a metal bar loaded with metal weights. The purpose is to see which entrant can lift the most weight. Though now popular in many places around the world, weightlifting first appeared in Europe, Egypt, Japan, and Turkey.

Equipment

A *barbell* is a long steel bar with wheels, or small *disks*, attached to each end. The bar is 7 feet, 2 inches (2.2 meters) long and weighs 4.4 pounds (20 kilograms). The disks are covered with rubber or plastic and are color-coded according to their weight.

Competitors stand on a 4.8-yard (4-meter) square platform that is covered with a nonslippery material. In addition to lifting boots, they wear costumes that cover the midsection and have two straps circling the shoulders.

The Event

Weightlifting uses two types of lifts. In the *snatch*, the athlete bends down, grabs the barbell, and lifts the bar above his or her head in one quick motion. The *clean and jerk* permits the lifter to rest the barbell at the shoulders before jerking it over the head. Contestants are allowed three attempts to succeed on each lift. After a successful lift, additional disks are added to increase the weight.

Powerlifting has three types of lifts. In the *squat*, they must lower to a squatting position with the barbell resting on their shoulders, then raise themselves to the upright position. In the *bench press*, the athlete lies on a bench, lowers the barbell to his or her chest, and pushes it up. With the *dead lift*, the athlete grabs the barbell

Russia's Andrei Chemerkin lifts the world record 457 kilograms (1,225 pounds) at the 1996 Summer Olympics.

off the floor, then lifts it above his or her head in one motion.

Contestants are grouped according to their weights. The Olympic Games, for instance, has nine classes, ranging from *featherweight* to *super heavyweight*.

Three referees decide if a lift has been performed properly. They announce either a *good lift* or a *no lift*. A no lift is called when the athlete includes any incorrect movements, such as pausing when not permitted or touching the barbell with the head. In a tie, the lifter who weighs less is declared the winner.

History

Weightlifting as it is structured today started in Western Europe in the nineteenth century, when lifters were a fixture of circuses. London, England, hosted the world's first championships in 1891, and the sport joined the Olympic Games in 1896. European and Egyptian lifters dominated the sport in its early years.

Weightlifting made significant gains in the United States when the sport was added to the Amateur Athletic Union in 1928. Following the end of World War II in 1945, the sport enjoyed a surge in participation. American weightlifters began offering solid competition to European and Egyptian athletes. American weightlifters quickly won twelve Olympic gold medals and set over fifty world records.

Since the 1960s, weightlifters from Russia (formerly the Soviet Union) and the United States have battled for supremacy. Russian Andrei Chemerkin set an Olympic record in 1996 by lifting 1,008 pounds (376 kilograms). Also in 1996, 119-pound Halil Muttu of Turkey lifted 633 pounds (236 kilograms), more than five times his body weight.

Wrestling

Wrestling is a sport in which two athletes attempt to overpower one another and *pin* (hold) the other person's shoulders to a mat. To accomplish this, a series of different holds are employed.

Equipment

The match is held on a cushioned *mat* made from canvas or synthetic material. A *center circle*, 39 inches (97.5 centimeters) in diameter, rests inside the central wrestling area, which extends to 22 feet 9 inches (6.8 meters) in diameter. Contestants wear headgear, a protective supporter, lightweight shoes, and a tight-fitting, one-piece outfit called a *singlet*.

The Event

In all forms of wrestling, the match begins with the contestants grasping each other in the *tie-up*. They then try to gain the advantage with a *takedown*, a maneuver in which the opponent is forced off balance and tossed to the ground. Maneuvers gaining control or escape earn the wrestler points. If one wrestler pins another, he wins the match. Otherwise, whichever contestant receives the most points in the match wins.

While more than fifty forms of wrestling exist around the world, the two most popular are *Greco-Roman* and *freestyle*. Greco-Roman wrestling, most popular in Europe, demands that the wrestler win by using only arm holds and upper body strength. Leg holds and trips are forbidden, as are holds below the waist.

Freestyle wrestling permits the use of legs to hold or lift an opponent and allows moves that Greco-Roman wrestling bans. This form of the sport is most popular at high schools and

Wrestlers are awarded points for takedowns, but must have his opponent on his back to earn a pin.

colles in the United States or as a strenuous form of exercise for anyone attempting to remain in good physical condition.

Wrestlers are divided into ten different weight *classes* ranging from 105.5 to 286 pounds (47.7 to 129.4 kilograms). Wrestlers in each weight class are paired with an opponent through a blind draw, and the top three finishers in the meet receive medals. Matches vary in length from three two-minute *periods* in high school to one five-minute period in international and Olympic wrestling.

History

People have been wrestling for thousands of years. French cave drawings fifteen-thousand to twenty-thousand years old include wrestlers.

Wrestlers withstand the most rigorous training program of any organized sport.

Hebrew and Sumerian scrolls prominently list the names of wrestling champions. Egyptian tombs include five-thousand-year-old wall paintings depicting the sport of wrestling. The famed ancient Greek poet Homer mentions wrestling in both the *Iliad* and the *Odyssey*.

Greek wrestling included the style that evolved into Greco-Roman wrestling as well as the *pancratium*, a brutal event that permitted almost any tactic. Greeks staged wrestling competitions to celebrate important events, and in 708 B.C., they included it as an Olympic event.

The Romans adopted the sport, and wrestling contests drew enthusiastic crowds during the Middle Ages.

Freestyle wrestling combined the pancratium with a wild form of wrestling practiced by Native Americans in the New World.

The Pancratium

The modern style of wrestling is nothing like one of its earliest versions. In ancient Greece athletes clashed in a contest called the pancratium, a combination of boxing and wrestling in which everything except eye gouging was permitted. A participant could bite, kick, or punch his opponent in these violent matches, which frequently ended in death.

Yacht Racing

Yacht racing is the sport of racing *yachts*, or sailboats, over predetermined courses. Yacht racing is popular throughout most parts of the globe.

Date of Origin	**1661**
Place of Origin	**England**
Legendary Performer	**Dennis Connor**
Governing Body	**International Yacht Racing Union**
Where They Compete	**Worldwide**
Championship Event	**America's Cup**

Equipment

Racing yachts can range from 11 feet (3.4 meters) to longer than 100 feet (30.7 meters) in length. They carry *anchors*, *sails*, and *flags*.

The courses selected for different races vary. A race committee familiar with local weather, tides, and wind determines the length and direction of the course. Some courses are laid out in triangular fashion and may be 1 to 2 miles long (1.6 to 3.2 kilometers), while others stretch hundreds of miles across the ocean.

The Event

Yachts compete with each other to get in the best position to cross the starting line at the signal. Should any craft edge over the *starting line* early, she must return and cross over it again. The yachts must round each *mark*, usually indicated by a buoy, in proper order and in a preestablished manner. If a yacht passes the mark on the wrong side, she must return by that side and correctly round the mark. The yacht with the fastest time completing the course wins the event.

Some races open competition to yachts of different sizes and designs, but to ensure fairness the boats are handicapped.

The first known yacht race occurred in England in 1661, when King Charles II defeated his brother, the Duke of York. In the United States, yachting received boosts from the New York Yacht Club and the Detroit Boat Club, both founded in the early 1800s.

Weather is a tremendous factor in yacht racing events.

180

Bibliography

American Red Cross. *Canoeing*. Garden City, N.Y.: Doubleday & Company, Inc., 1977.

Arlott, John. Editor. *The Oxford Companion to World Sports & Games*. London: Oxford University Press, 1975.

Associated Press and Grolier. *Pursuit of Excellence: The Olympic Story*. Danbury, Conn.: Grolier Enterprises Inc., 1979.

Bishop, George, and Shaun Barrington. *Encyclopedia of Motorcycling*. New York: Smithmark Publishers Inc., 1995.

Brondfield, Jerry. *Great Moments in American Sports*. New York: Random House, 1974.

Broido, Bing. *Spalding Book of Rules*. Indianapolis, Ind.: Masters Press, 1993.

Clark, Patrick. *Sports Firsts*. New York: Facts on File, Inc., 1981.

Darden, Anne. *The Sports Hall of Fame*. New York: Drake Publishers Inc., 1976.

The Diagram Group. *Rules of the Game*. New York: Paddington Press, 1974.

The Diagram Group. *The Rule Book*. New York: St. Martin's Press, 1983.

Durant, John. *Highlights of the Olympics*. New York: Hastings House Publishers, 1964.

Editors of Macmillan Publishing Company. *The Baseball Encyclopedia*. New York: Macmillan Publishing Company, 1990.

Editors of Merriam-Webster. *Webster's Sports Dictionary*. Springfield, Mass.: G. & C. Merriam Company, Publishers, 1976.

Editors of *Sports Illustrated. 1999 Sports Almanac*. New York: Bishop Books, 1998.

Editors of Time-Life. *Yesterday in Sport*. New York: Time-Life Books, 1968.

Fisher, David, and Reginald Bragonier, Jr. *What's What in Sports*. Maplewood, N.J.: Hammond Incorporated, 1984.

Fleischer, Nat, and Sam Andre. *A Pictorial History of Boxing*. London: Hamlyn, 1983.

Frommer, Harvey. *Olympic Controversies*. New York: Franklin Watts, 1987.

Garber, Angus G. III. *Champions! The Greatest Sports Legends of All time*. New York: Mallard Press, 1990.

Grimsley, Will. *101 Greatest Athletes of the Century*. New York: Bonanza Books, 1987.

Hanlon, Thomas. *The Sports Rule Book*. Champaign, Ill.: Human Kinetics, 1998.

Henry, Bill, and Patricia Henry Yeomans. *An Approved History of the Olympic Games*. Los Angeles, Calif.: The Southern California Committee for the Olympic Games, 1984.

Hickok, Ralph. *The Encyclopedia of North American Sports History*. New York: Facts On File, 1992.

Hills, Gavin. *All Action Skateboarding*. Minneapolis, Minn.: Lerner Publications Company, 1992.

Hoare, Syd. *Judo*. Lincolnwood, Ill.: NTC Publishing Group, 1993.

Hodges, David. *Great Racing Drivers*. New York: Arco Publishing Company, Inc., 1966.

Hollander, Phyllis. *American Women in Sports*. New York: Grosset & Dunlap, Inc., 1972.

Jensen, Julie. *Beginning Snowboarding*. Minneapolis, Minn.: Lerner Publications Company, 1996.

Kendall, Brian. *100 Great Moments in Hockey*. New York: Viking Press, 1994.

LaBlanc, Michael, and Richard Henshaw. *The World Encyclopedia of Soccer*. Detroit, Mich.: Visible Ink, 1994.

LeMond, Greg, and Ken Gordis. *Greg LeMond's Complete Book of Bicycling*. New York: G.P. Putnam's Sons, 1987.

Malone, John. *The Encyclopedia of Figure Skating*. New York: Facts On File, Inc., 1998.

McWhirter, Norris. *Guinness Book of Sports Records, Winners, & Champions*. New York: Sterling Publishing Co., Inc., 1982.

Menke, Frank G. *The Encyclopedia of Sports*. New York: A.S. Barnes and Company, 1969.

Millar, Cam. *In-Line Skating Basics*. New York: Sterling Publishing Co., Inc., 1996.

Needham, Richard. Editor. *Ski Magazine's Encyclopedia of Skiing*. New York: Harper & Row, Publishers, 1979.

Postman, Andrew, and Larry Stone. *The Ultimate Book of Sports Lists*. New York: Bantam Books, 1990.

Schaap, Dick. *An Illustrated History of the Olympics*. New York: Alfred A. Knopf, 1975.

Searle, Caroline, and Bryn Vaile. *The IOC Official Olympic Companion 1996*. London: Brassey's Sports, 1996.

U.S. Olympic Committee. *Barcelona Albertville 1992*. Salt Lake City, Utah: Mikko Laitinen, 1992.

Wallechinsky, David. *The Complete Book of the Olympics*. New York: Penguin Books, 1984.

Weiskopf, Herm, and Chuck Pezzano. *Sports Illustrated Bowling*. New York: Winner's Circle Books, 1987.

Index